Bread & Molasses

ANDY MacDONALD

Stoddart

First published in 1976 by Musson Book Company

Canadian Cataloguing in Publication Data

MacDonald, Andy.
  Bread & molasses

ISBN 0-7737-0030-7 bd.
ISBN 0-7737-1009-4 pa.

1. MacDonald, Andy. I. Title.

CT310.M2414A3   971.5'04'0924   C76-017012-6

Published in 1986 by
Stoddart Publishing Co. Limited
34 Lesmill Road
Don Mills, Ontario M3B 2T6

8th Printing — February 1986

Hardcover ISBN 0-7737-0030-7
Softcover ISBN 0-7737-1009-4
Printed and bound in Canada

I dedicate this to my daughter Dianne, whose help was invaluable to the completion of the book.

Contents

One   **Home and Family/1**

Two   **School Days/8**

Sam and the Urinal
The Little Brown Book In the Puddle
Someone Has Stolen Africa
Why Would a Word Be Going To Paris?
Young Lochinvar
The Day Santa Turned Into a Barn Rat
The Soup Spoon
The Pit Mit Stew

Three   **Pa's Saving Ways/31**

Always Sexily Attired
The Sexy Bathers
The Crows
The Tasty Fig
The Floating Blueberries

Four   **Christmas Capers/50**

Oh, My Poor Duck
I'm Jack Spratt, But She's Too Fat
Who Can That Be Under the Robe?
Bob Skates Aren't For Swimming
The Expanding Pipe
This Cardboard Duck Is Delicious

Five   **The Few Times We Weren't Sick,
We Were Accident-Prone/61**

    Acute Asphyxiation, Aged Nine
    Teedy's Tongue
    You Broke My Back
    The Dwarf Is Under the Covers With Me
    Sulphur and Molasses
    Salt Porking Fad

Six   **Boonies, Lamps, Freezing Pipes, and
Coal Stoves/71**

    The Night Billy Cooked the Pot
    The Double-Holer
    Don't Spit On the Lamp
    Oh, To Be a Camel, So We Could Fill Our Humps

Seven   **Our Adventures With the Animal
Kingdom/79**

    The Sad Death
    You Smell Like Wet Feathers
    The Unclucked Hen
    Playing Cow
    Catch Her On the Squat
    The Purified Pig
    I Was Attacked By a Dead Pig

Eight   **With Ma's Death Come Stricter
Rules, Ghosts, and Other Means
Of Acquiring Food/91**

    Things Change Swiftly
    The Bunny Rabbit Woman

The Brothers, Grim, Become Housekeepers
That Great Grabbing Feeling
The Day Dida Died
Out We Go Again
The Night Billy Burglarized Pa
The Bouncy Walk
Lunch Time At the Wakes
The Delicious Pound Party
Eating Again?

Nine   **All For One and One For All**/111

Tobacco Pudding Clubhouse
Eat, Drink, and Be Mousey
The Skeleton's Last Stand

Ten   **Sex and the Single Tooth**/119

Amy Took Ma's Trinkets To Boston
Look Bill, No Teeth
There's a Tooth In My Egg
I Was a Painted Bag
Six Cents, Just To See the Back Of Her Head
Free Burlesque

Eleven **The Executioner and Job Jinx**/131

The Strangled Rooster
Follow the Flies
Rinso Sausage

One

Home and Family

Sydney Mines is a small coal-mining town on Cape Breton Island. During mining hours black smoke bellows out of tall blast furnaces, giving the surrounding countryside the tired, sooty look of all mining towns. I was born here into a family of eleven, and I guess we were lucky to have survived the hungry thirties, getting by on Pa's meagre cheque from the mine, Ma's saving ways, and whatever we kids managed to come by in our end of town.

Our end of town was Shore Road, the street next to the harbour. It was on this street that we lived. Below our house billows of black smoke poured from the chimneys of the coal mine. The only thing that settled the coal dust was when the 5 p.m. whistle shrieked. Then we were on guard for our Pa who would be home directly.

Separating our house from the harbour was a small field, which ended in a cliff that dropped eighty feet to the water below. It provided a lovely view in summertime as we watched huge coal boats pass by on their way to pick up bunker coal at the Sydney Pier. As their haunting whistles filled the air, we'd look across two-and-one-half miles of quiet water to Sydney and dream that some day we too would own cars like the rich, who travelled wherever they pleased.

Along the edge of the cliffs, our square red house stood out like a giant amidst dwarfs, being a storey higher than the other houses in line with it. The red giant that housed us was built by Pa and looked like Pa, stern and strict. It held thirteen of us, my mother and father, five girls and six boys.

Pa had built four bedrooms upstairs, one of which was occupied by him and Ma. Our five sisters were in one of the larger ones, two older brothers in a smaller room, and the four youngest boys were put in an unfinished room, where we slept two, three, and sometimes four in a bed. We could easily forecast the weather in winter by the depth of frost on the nail ends that poked through from the tar paper on the outer roof.

In the upstairs hall there was a coal cookstove with a stovepipe that we had to duck under before entering our rooms. This stove was used only for heating in winter. Once Billy got into a lot of trouble with Pa when, by accident, something of his got cooked that just shouldn't have.

At the top of the stairs was a picture of a boat caught in the ice. It was cold enough in the house in winter without having that picture staring you in the eye on your way to bed. On one wall at the head of the stairs was a small little window, which we used as a lookout against Pa's unexpected returns—always catching us in some kind of deviltry.

A mini hall and fifteen steps took you down to the first floor, where a small hallway was interrupted by a big front room, which was, as Teedy the youngest boy put it, "not too rid of ghosts". There was a small fireplace in this room, which sent its heat mostly up the chimney. We had to pass this spooky room to get to the kitchen, and we became so adept at passing it swiftly we could have given lessons on how to do it.

It was the kitchen that was the heart of the house. No matter how little food we had, Ma, when she was alive, always managed to have something boiling and bubbling on the cookstove, which staved off our hunger pangs, at least for a while. The large coal stove was always going, not only to keep the porridge pot hot, but also to lend heat to the rest of the house.

We always seemed to be clustered around the long kitchen table, either to eat or, when the dishes were cleared away and

2

Pa was in the picture, to pretend to be studying our lessons while Pa read his newspaper and puffed on his pipe.

There was a dining-room to the right of the kitchen, which might as well not have been there, as it was too cold to use in the winter and in summer the only time we ate there was when we had company.

Off the kitchen was a dingy little porch, which held flour, molasses, tea, and foods that wouldn't freeze. In winter the door from the porch to the kitchen was opened and shut in seconds. Unwanted was the neighbour who came rushing in leaving the door open. The gush of wind would blow out the kerosene lamp flame and all of us would run to Ma for shelter until it was lit again.

Ma was always the one who protected us and took up for us in everything, unknown to Pa. Pa belonged to the Masons, and when he was out late to his meetings, we never worried whether or not he'd get home safely. But if Ma was gone for just a few minutes, we four brothers and baby Pearl would cry and wail, saying it was so dark she'd probably get lost. A heavy weight would be lifted from our hearts when we heard her footsteps, and we'd all go to sleep with dampened eyes.

Ma always cushioned the blows from Pa.

Pa, on the other hand, was a strict disciplinarian. A powerful five-foot-ten and weighing over two hundred pounds, we heard many stories of his strength from men who worked with him in the mines. Day after day Pa worked hard in the mines to provide for us, but we had to abide faithfully to the rules he set down. With his mathematical mind he always knew how to buy the cheapest and best food for his large brood. He'd buy in quantities— one hundred pounds of flour and meat, and fish in hundred pound lots, too. Nothing was to be wasted. No second helpings at the table.

Our menu for the week was as follows: Monday, salt herring and potatoes; Tuesday, codfish; Wednesday, our ration of steak; Thursday, the other half-dozen salt herring (I hated them and still do); Friday, codfish again; Saturday, beans all day long (and they talk about a gas shortage today). Sunday

3

meant porridge for breakfast (with four teaspoons sugar if Pa wasn't around and level one if he was present), egg for dinner, and the last of the left-over beans for supper. None of this was in abundance.

Now, eating at the table with Pa was no easy thing. It was similar to waiting for your murder sentence to be handed down. Manners were always on your mind. Sometimes you'd slip and place an elbow on the table. That was all he needed. You were charged and condemned to bed that very moment without your supper.

Our clothing was also rationed, and God help the brother who didn't take extremely good care of his clothes. But Pa sometimes carried his strictness too far, like the time he caught brother Billy wearing his Sunday clothes on a weekday. The next day, Pa sent Billy to school with a dress on.

I don't remember too much about the girls as they all left home first, except for red-haired Pearl, the youngest. The two older boys went away to work, so that left Billy, Murray (my twin), Teedy, Pearl, and me at home.

Billy, as I recall, was the best fighter in the family, willing to tackle anything or anyone. He was also a born salesman and a real ladies man. He was sure he could charm them and usually did. Sometimes it annoyed us that he always got the girls. He was the type who was appointed president or vice-president of organizations, and he had a knack for looking you right in the eye and lying. You knew he wasn't telling the truth, yet you still believed him. I think he hypnotized you.

Billy could get along with Pa better than the rest of us and took a lot of chances we never would have. One time after Ma died, Pa received a pure white hand-made pullover from a matron in the hospital for a Christmas present. Billy somehow got hold of the sweater and dyed it red. Pa never knew what became of it. Then Billy, decked out in the red pullover, would help Pa search high and low for the white sweater, until finally Pa discontinued the hunt as a lost cause.

The one thing I remember about Murray, my twin, was how saving he was. Once when he was about eight years old he had scarlet fever. He was a mess, had lost about ten pounds, and a big lump even came out under his throat. Everyone felt sorry for him and kept dropping change into his bank. One day, Freddy, an older brother, asked him if he wanted an ice cream. Murray said yes and when Freddy went to take the nickel from his piggy bank, Murray almost went crazy with rage. Freddy had to put it back and buy it with his own money.

Murray was also very wiry. One day Pa caught him climbing up a telephone pole and bellowed for him to come down. Murray got caught on the guide wire and couldn't move. Pa thought he was defying him and gave the guide wire a great shake, sending Murray with the rear end ripped out of his pants plummeting to the ground like a monkey leaping from a tree.

One of Murray's weaker points, though, was his breath— an aged sewer would have been easier to live with. But we had to put up with the odour as he was having trouble with his baby teeth—all rotten. This must have been the reason for the stench. Many a night the rest of us, sleeping in the same bed with him, would keep our noses fully covered, smothering rather than face that smell. Once, a friend visiting my mother held the cute cuddly Murray in her lap until she got a whiff of his breath. She pushed him roughly from her, saying to my mother, "Agnes, take this child, he's been eating shit."

Murray wasn't the only one who should have used Scope. Teedy, the youngest of the boys, also had troubles along this line when he had his tonsils out. They should have isolated him from human beings. If we could have just looked at him without having him talk to us; but he always had some sad story to tell, like how sick he was and how the nurses had sent him home (he was terribly lonesome for Ma). They were glad to get rid of his putrid breath.

The trick was to keep Teedy's conversations short. We even suggested he gargle creolin, and he was about to take us up on it when an older sister told him he would die an instant death. It wasn't long though before he was giving off a better odour;

and then like a sick hen that has recovered, he was thrown in with the rest of us, and we weren't long taking a bite of his candy as his breath was clear again.

Teedy always seemed to be sick and fevered, with an aspirin in one hand and Niter in the other. (Niter was used for fevers, but now they give it to horses.) Maybe that's why I picked him to tell my secrets to, thinking that he wouldn't last too long and would take my secrets with him to the grave. One day I came upon some freshly dug earth twenty feet from the cliffs and convinced I had come upon a newly buried treasure I rushed to tell Teedy. Back we ran and dug as fast as we could. At last the box came into view. I kept looking around to make sure no one was coming. We didn't want to share this with anyone. We grasped the box and hauled it up onto the ground. We couldn't open the lid fast enough. Finally, the box opened, we both peered inside and the sound "Aghghgh" came from our lips. Inside lay Patty McLean, a dog we had evaded for years because it had T.B. (It must have had it because the whole family did.) We were so scared of catching this dread disease, we didn't even close the box and cleared out of there in a hurry.

Convinced we had caught T.B. from the dog, we spit for two months afterwards.

Then came the youngest in the family, Pearl. Along with plenty of red hair and freckles, she also had plenty of mouth. But she was the baby and we loved her.

Pearl had a nipple off an old nursing bottle that she used to suck herself to sleep with each night. Without that pacifier she would howl for hours. One night when Ma and Pa were visiting friends, Pearl lost her nipple. We could hear her crying and sent Teedy upstairs to tend to her. He never came back and so we went up to see what was keeping him. There he was with his finger in Pearl's mouth. Every time he made a move to pull it out, she'd start screeching again. We told him to stay there all night to keep her quiet, but after a couple of hours sucking on Teedy's tired finger, she went to sleep for the night.

As a family we got along rather smoothly, unless Pa was around. There wasn't much squabbling amongst us kids as in most families. I guess we were too terrified of what Pa would do if he caught us; and we were all great pals with each other, kind of the way people band together when a war is on.

Two

School Days

Then came school, and another war began in our life. Our Concentration Camp school couldn't have been built in a more gruesome location. A huge two-storey, square, red brick building, it was almost in line with the Town Hall, which housed the jail. We never turned our heads much towards the jail as we always had guilty consciences about the secret crimes we had committed.

The school halls were dark and stuffy, and lining each side of the halls were nails upon which hung long, outdated coats. These dingy halls were used as dungeons for misbehaving kids. When the teacher came to bring you in after serving your time out there, she'd have quite a job to find you as you'd be tangled up in someone's long coat praying for air.

Murray and I were sentenced to school when we were four. The grind had started, and we were soon convinced that we couldn't stand too much of it. They seated us together, and I would look at Murray and yawn and he'd look at me and yawn. We were yawning for Ma.

That night we both decided that in order to get out of school, any ploy fair or foul was legitimate in view of the horrors of the prison life we were facing. So the next day we packed our little bag and left for school, wondering if our plan was going to work. We were soon settled into our double desk, and after half an hour Murray begins to smear his eyes with spit—putting it on thick and sticky. Our teacher that year happened to be a very nice lady with a soft spot for new kids at school. She comes over and nudges Murray's shoulders. His head bounces up and comes down with a thud.

"What's the matter with Murray?" the teacher asks.

"He's sick," I answer pathetically.

"Well, you'd better go home, Murray," she says, quite concerned. This was Murray's cue. Eyes dripping with spit, he groans, "Please, Miss, I don't know the way." Which was fair enough as we did live two miles away.

"Do you know the way, Andy?"

"Yes, Miss."

"Then you had better take Murray home."

The spit sham worked wonderfully for nearly a whole term, the two of us switching sick roles every now and then. I still can't figure out why the teacher was so gullible. If one of us went, the other automatically followed. When we left the classroom, we'd walk slowly and sickly like walking wounded until out of sight of the school, and then rush off to play.

Of course it wasn't all hookey— we had to at least keep up appearances. Those rare times we were in attendance there were a number of problems: one of these was lunch. We took our lunches in a small paper bag (at one time an onion bag) that was opened and closed more frequently than old Santa's sack, until by accident someone would either take it to start a fire or use it for toilet paper. When we did manage to preserve our lunches, our pride dictated that we did not eat with the upper classes. No wonder, since lunch always consisted of three slices of bread, drenched in molasses and soaked right through. Cookies were scarce. On the rare occasions on which I actually attended school, Murray and I would eat out of the same bag. Usually he would have it all to himself. Murray was more conscientious about attendance than I was.

One time we had found a hiding place in the basement to

eat our meagre lunch when we were interrupted by the boot-legger's son. This kid just didn't belong with us. First of all he had a lunch can. And inside he had a thermos bottle, wax-pa-pered meat sandwiches, an apple, and an orange— and I'll never forget the sight of the chocolate marshmallow cookies that lined the top of his can.

We were just getting ready to munch our own stuff, when the intruder threw a quick smirk at our lunch of molasses-stained bread. Murray, always ready to tackle anything, grabbed the guy's can, and we divided his lunch between us, generously tossing our little wrinkled bag at him. It was the nicest lunch we ever ate at school.

Sam and the Urinal
The first year of school was tricky for about seventy-five per cent of the kids who had never experienced inside toilets be-fore. We had seen toilets in the movies, but had never seen urinals.

As I said before, our school was like a concentration camp with its overbearing laws and the students talking in petrified whispers. To go to the toilet, you raised your hand with a sort of waving motion, done only from the wrist. Others wouldn't even bother raising a hand after seeing yours dangling there for nearly ten minutes. The teacher usually saw you as soon as you slapped it up, but why she never realized that you were in great pain and that the human bladder can only stand so much pressure I'll never know.

Anyhow, I decided this one time to change hands. This is a tricky thing to do as the sudden shift of the spine, if you can imagine the bladder to be a bowl three-quarters full of water, almost spills the contents over the edge of the bowl. My arm is still dangling in the air. I don't use the wave I started out with— can't afford to. Now comes the last movement the blad-der will allow— I cross my legs. Across the aisle, the dentist's daughter slips up a clean small arm with a beautiful Bulova wrist watch. I just have time to notice the watch, then the teacher says, "Yes, Alma," and Alma takes the words right out of my mouth: "Please Miss, may I leave the room?" "Yes you may, Alma." Here I am bursting, both arms useless from dangling and counting my fingers and thumbs for nearly an hour. Disgusted, I take my hands down. There are other ways to milk a cat. Now my mind is working in desperation. I have on this heavy underwear I haven't changed for three weeks. It's bulky. Can I risk aiming for the bulk portions of the legs? It's 2 p.m. I should be dried off by 3:30 p.m. My mind is made up. It's sink or swim. A wave of relief passes over me. Alma is back, dry as a wooden God. But it's too late. I feel as though someone tossed me into a wishing well.

I'll never forget the first day in Grade One. A kid named Sam shot up his frail holey-sweatered arm to leave the room. The teacher must have realized the urgent answer he needed, and so away Sam rushed to the toilet.

This was at 2, and at 3 p.m. Sam was nowhere in sight. Had someone dognapped him, as he had on furry pants? Or perhaps he'd turned old and had a gout seizure. As usual I had my paw up to leave, when the teacher looked at me seriously and said, "What's happened to Sam?" Now even in Grade One, they would never allow two males to go to the bathroom at once. I don't know if they thought we had sexual activities in mind or what. As far as Sam went, I sat beside him in school and his clothes always smelt like they were damp and his breath was like a pulp mill— there was no need to be worried.

I guess she was desperate to know what had happened to Sam because she said, "Please go see what's keeping Sam, Andy." I felt like an ambulance driver in front of the class. Up I hopped and went straight to the bathroom. After what I saw, I should have taken the whole class down to the bathroom to clean Sam up.

Sam hadn't made it to the toilets. His biggest problem was those damn braces. One of the braces was fastened to the flap button on his underwear. There he was trying to straddle a urinal, tied up in braces and underwear to such an extent that he looked like an acrobat. The urinals were quite high off the floor and Sam was very short. He kept jerking his little body up to try and sit on it, and with every jerk his braces would snap against him. And on top of this he had diarrhea. He looked at me in a pathetic manner as if I was his mother. I wouldn't have squealed on him, but he looked so smelly and dirty I was disgusted with him and said, "Sam, I'm going to tell the teacher you crapped in the urinal."

This was a big mistake on my part because in disentangling him from the urinal, he gave a heaving sigh, threw both hands around me, and I was in one hell of a mess. There wasn't an inch of him that was clean. I kept trying to pry his smelly hands from my body, but he was like a drowning person clinging to me. Eventually I got him calmed down.

I went upstairs without Sam. I think the teacher could smell me and knew what was up when I told her Sam was in an awful mess, because she didn't press the subject too much. What I should have said was, "Listen teacher, that boy's rotten, and if you place that little hunk of stink in my seat next to me when he comes up, I'm leaving school forever." Sam arrived upstairs just as the class was marching out, and he fell into line as quickly as he fell in the urinal. A quick glance told me Sam had his braces buttoned wrong again, but I wouldn't have told him for the world as I would have ended up having to straighten them.

Why hadn't teachers shown us toilets and urinals in those days? Some of us weren't too brave about flushing a toilet, thinking we'd go slushing down too. They never explained anything to us. We had to pick our own way. And I know Sam would have made the urinal if he'd had a straight movement and a belt on; but diarrhea and braces don't mix. I'll bet any money on the slickest guy.

The Little Brown Book In the Puddle

Another problem we had was our reader. Murray and I had to share a reader. Pa would examine it daily to see that it was being well taken care of. It had a sort of brown table cloth cover to it, and if even a drop of water ever fell on it, it would leave a very noticeable stain. I can't describe the fear we felt that day the flap on our school-bag flew open and our reader plopped into a mud puddle. What would Pa do to us? We were pretty green in those early days, and we never thought of simply painting the entire cover with dark brown paint— so all we could do was to hide the reader from Pa for the whole term.

It was almost compulsory for the teacher to grade Murray and me at the same time, because if only one of us went ahead it meant the added expense of a second reader. Murray and I made it through Grades One, Two, and Three together— but the blow fell the next year when I was graded, leaving Murray and both my next-door buddies behind in a different school. It was a drastic semester for me. I couldn't get used to the new environment. And to make matters worse, I fell into the clutches of the most hateful teacher who ever taught. This did little to improve my love of school. I figured, "Lady, you're not going to see much of me."

So the fun began. I attended school maybe three or four days each month. The rest of the time was spent along the shores and high cliffs near our house. My biggest worry at the time was to keep my absence from older brothers and sisters who went to the same school. I doctored this up with some clever timing. I'd stand on a high ledge, which gave me a good view of our house, and wait for the noise and traffic of kids coming home from school, singing and playing, and join right in—just as though I had been right in there slogging away with them all day long. The trick was to be as discreet as possible, eat well, and pretend to be a good little schoolboy who had just come home from an enjoyable day of learning.

The other thing that helped was that Pa was completely mixed up with all the report cards what with ten other kids around the house— so he never knew whether he'd signed mine or not. It was now June, and report card season was buzzing. But I never got one because one of my best friends had told the teacher that I'd quit Grade Four. The teacher had seized my belongings, which consisted of a slate with scratches on it, a V for Victory sign broken out in the corner, and a slate pencil. Fortunately for me, Pa at this time had been hurt in the mine. This came as a blessing as he was in a cast all summer and couldn't get at me too fast.

In any event, my honest waiting for Murray and my two buddies to catch up with me paid off, and they were graded right into my truant arms. We all signed up together the following fall. I was still far superior in knowledge, however, as I had had at least eight days of the previous four semesters.

Murray, as I said, became pretty conscientious about school. And that year he was indispensible to my career in hookey. He would tell the teacher that I was sick or away—whatever made her feel good. We had a pretty soft teacher that year, but I did build up my batting average from eight days to about twenty since Pa's back was on the mend and the smell of report cards was again in the air.

Then Billy found an unused report card somewhere. Whenever Pa got the urge to see my report card, I'd dress this one up, put in some good marks, plus days present, and proudly pass it on to Pa, who almost burst with pride at his genius son. God help me if he had ever found out.

Pa was always very critical about report cards. Perhaps his days as a school-teacher accounted for his strictness. Our report card had to be A-1 for Pa to sign. Unfortunately, we used to have one teacher in particular who was an evil beast. She knew how strict Pa was and would go out of her way to phone him up. She'd tell him you hadn't been there that morning, that you'd received twenty-seven per cent in English, and anything else that would kindle the fire. So even though the phone was considered a luxury in those days, more often than not it meant disaster for us. After a few rough lessons in electronics, however, I was able to disconnect any incoming calls that might jeopardize my character. Little wads of chewed-up paper were poked under the bell on top of the phone, pushed in, and packed tightly. The phone would ring but there was no sound. This went on for almost a full term. I was learning more from hookey than anything at school.

All was well until one evening in the spring when Pa was going up to bed. He took a right wheel at the bottom of the stairs when he noticed the bells going wild with no noise coming from them. He reached in, pulled out fifty spit-balls, and answered the call— coincidentally Teedy's teacher wondering why he hadn't attended school for a week. If only I had known Teedy was playing hookey too that week, I'd have put in some extra balls for him and throttled the phone for good. Ted's sentence was particularly heavy that time. Pa pushed him backwards into a large empty coal hod after the call. He landed in the hod bottom first and answered all Pa's questions from that position. It took two of us to pry him loose— to serve a sentence imposed by Pa to go to bed every afternoon at 4 p.m. throughout the summer. Today, forty years later, he's the only brother who looks rested.

My father, who was working in the coal mine from 5 a.m. to 5 p.m. daily to give us a good education, didn't like to hear that we weren't taking advantage of it.

As I said, report card season was always a tense time. Our reports always seemed to jump with bad marks. Judgements were marked with an X on the right-hand side of the card. "Promotion in danger" was marked in erasible ink curiously enough. I often attempted to erase that particular X, only to disfigure it and make it even more conspicuous than ever. The comment "Times tardy" to Pa was the main artery of a student's intentions. But our intentions were good— it was just that we despised school. "Whispers too much" to Pa meant: "He's a villain, murderer, and rapist." If there hadn't been that perpetual X beside "Whispers too much" each term I could have relaxed a little, but I was never fortunate enough to have a blank there.

This was invariably followed by "Appears not to try", which may have been true in a sense, but why rub it in? Another was "Seldom does well". This was untrue. I did all right playing truant three times a week, and the other guys thought I did everything just fine. "Work shows a falling off." This made us feel we were getting old and senile and that we

15

would have to make up for lost time by getting in some good solid playing.

Looking further down the card you'd see "Comes poorly prepared". We didn't know whether this referred to our learning or our attire. We took it as an insult as we'd usually have on odd-coloured socks, cheap old pants, with a woollen sweater for underwear— legs through the armholes— and a shirt buttoned up wrong. "Rude— discourteous at times" was another favourite. Were we rude? We wouldn't have bothered a louse, and there were plenty around in those days. But who could be happy when you arrived in school (if you had bothered to go that day) to face the orangutang with her new blouse on and her arms all greased up for her usual scrapping with the stupid kids. Looking at an old-necked teacher, shuffling about with a geography book in her hand, wasn't for us. She never asked any of the smart kids where Asia was situated: she would inevitably pick on the sleepy, stupid kids —who didn't even know which street the school was on. How I used to wish that I was an old man in my eighties— deaf, blind, and unbalanced— so that she would say in a sweet voice: "Sir, you had really better go home; it's such a nice day, and you really ought to take it easy." How your nerves would quiver when she bellowed at the class about the sins of truancy. About how you had time to fool around all week and never give a thought to geography or some such nonsense. I never condemned her for telling the truth, but why she had to tell the whole class at the top of her lungs when we only lived two miles away from school I'll never know. With Pa's sensitive ears he was liable to hear her. Of course we'd look repentant, thinking all the while: "Shut up you long-necked, no-lipped gannet!" After all it was bad enough having the screeching seagulls giving away your hideout on the cliffs near the house without her squawking.

"Annoys others" was another delightful comment. Who were we annoying? We were all sitting alone. And you didn't move your head to the left, right, or behind you. Always straight ahead. How could you annoy anyone when all you

were doing was sitting there with a secret eye on the clock
and thinking all the while: "I was a fool to come today. I have
so many outside interests."

"Copies too much." Pa always loved that one. And the old
bag's skinny arm loved marking an X beside it. Copies? The
kids who played hookey were all placed in separate seats
whenever they happened to drop in from their various fur-
loughs. Most times the desks around us were empty anyway.
You'd need telescopic eyes and a neck like a giraffe to even get
a peek at the blackboard, let alone copy your neighbour's ef-
forts. The teacher probably figured as much, but she enjoyed
torment: keeping the truants for a couple of hours after
school—hookers with no pay for overtime. And anyway it
didn't do her any good keeping us there with our noses in
some crusty old Latin text, as I'd always be conjuring up new
plans in retaliation: "I'll take four days off this week to recover
from the smell of lead and shellac, which is presently making
me throw up."

I always had an excuse.

Someone Has Stolen Africa
I remember the day I was finally forced to school through sor-
did circumstance after a number of weeks absence. The sick-
ening morning was soon upon me. My main concern was to
avoid questioning on all those lessons I had missed since the
last time I had dropped in. All the kids that day were looking
eager and keen with books at the ready and lessons prepared.
I hadn't even a pencil, let alone a book. I had unfortunately left
my books on the shore on a large rock, never dreaming that
the tide would come in that far.

In any case,the old teacher was in particularly good form
this morning and could barely refrain from throwing a few
barbs my way before the class had assembled. Her remarks
were getting pretty stale by now anyway. "Why here's our little visitor coming to see us. His father must be home today."
The old crab was definitely psychic. With all sixty pupils
looking on, she was positively gleeful about my embarrass-

ment. I didn't deserve this. I had just dropped by to see how the guys and gals were getting on. I figured my return made the day a bit more exciting for the kids. They seemed to enjoy my surprise visits and my dogfights with the teacher.

Anyone with any sense would definitely not ask a greenhorn like me the latest up-to-date questions on the various subjects. But just in case they did, I would always do my best to sit behind someone— girl or boy— with a wide head. Wonderful camouflage. If you were agile you could keep out of sight behind the kid's head. It was usually pretty effective for keeping out of sight from the teacher. So there I was that day after things had calmed down a bit after the initial drubbing, bobbing to the left and then to the right as the kid in front moved— her neck and my spine magically joined just like the song "Me and My Shadow". My bobbing went well for a while until the old goat up front caught on. The girl with the wide head and I had been doing remarkably well, until my cover was blown by an ungodly cough. I almost broke my neck trying to follow her coughing spasm. The old crow was on me in a flash. "Well, there's Andy bobbing around like a prize monkey. Go to the board, Andy." This was most unfair as I had been too involved studying rhythm and movement for the last half-hour to be concerned with the lesson at hand. Also, my dress was bound to bring ridicule from the sixty kids as I stood at the blackboard. So as I'm shuffling up there, I'm also wondering about what socks I have on. Which won't show, thank God, because I've got my gum rubbers on— but what about my sweater with the hole in the centre and the three cuffs on each arm?

Anyway, I was given a pointer to outline the boundaries of Africa on this map hanging there. After a few minutes of standing and swaying, the pointer begins to look the size of a toothpick. Where the hell is Africa anyway? No comment from the teacher and just the odd snicker from the inevitable smart kid. Five minutes in the same spot. Silence. My, how time flies. I manage to locate the Atlantic Ocean. But Africa? I almost broke down and suggested that it just wasn't on the map. I even discovered little Malta and felt that I should at least have received some praise for that discovery. Now my back was beginning to give, my legs were wobbly, my stomach sick, and my vision almost nil. I was going blind straining my eyes on the old map. I felt like saying, "Please Miss, I'm gravely ill and sort of blind." After feebly searching in vain for anything with the letter A, the old gal suddenly came rushing at me like a Fundy tide. What a chance she took, what with me standing there with the pointer in my hand. She grabbed my hand and tried to force it to Africa. I almost fell on my face at that point, off balance, trying stubbornly to keep the pointer on comforting little Malta. It may have been a great show for the class, but I'm sure I lost any potential girlfriends that day then and there.

Then suddenly my eyes focused on Africa. No wonder I couldn't find it— it takes up half the map. I begin to feel cocky about it all. Who says I'm stupid— there's Africa and she didn't even have to show me. She had tried, but I hadn't been ready to leave Malta.

Silence again. Then suddenly: "Well, where is it bounded?" "Oh," I say to myself, "don't you know that? Waiting all these years for me to tell you, and me so much younger than you." I knew bounded meant situated but had no idea by what land or water. She yells at the top of her lungs: "On the east by...." The class is beginning to get restless. I'm under considerable mental stress and pressure. I'm thinking: "Where in the name of God is the East?— no sun (the shades are all pulled), no compass. Here I am in the frozen North looking for the mild East. Maybe there's a typographical error on the map. Why won't Malta do?"

Then all of a sudden I get this blinding flash of inspiration and holler: "Africa is bounded on the east by the Red Sea." Everyone is quiet. I was expecting to get an old boot in the face, and so I wait for a yell but nothing happens. I go on: "And on the west by the Atlantic Ocean." That was easy enough. Now for the north and south. South Africa saves me in one direction, and I squeak through with "the Mediterranean on the north". I then hear a thump and figure the teacher must have fainted. No such luck, but she is pretty astonished nevertheless. Just as I am about to repair to my wide-headed friend, I hear: "How about exports? What does Africa export?" I am getting all kinds of help from the class now, but they are all muttering different items. I am on a forty-five degree slant trying to catch something, when I think I hear "coal". So I take a long shot and say "coal". Silence. I wait for a response, and after a minute or so she speaks up thoughtfully: "Well, it would export coal to a certain extent, I suppose." Hell, I'm teaching her something she never knew. Then she says: "And what else?" Immediate prompting from all sixty kids at once. They're getting really impatient by now. I'm trying my damnedest to catch some more items when the old crab's voice screeches through above the din telling me to return to my seat and to have the lesson prepared for the next day.

Not only did she despise me, but so did everyone else in the class by that time. Daggers everywhere. I could tell I wasn't wanted, and so I never attended any more sessions that term.

Why Would a Word Be Going To Paris?

After breathing in the salt air all day on my hookey stints, I would be starving. Home for lunch, I'd find a sister with the old washing machine out, a bunch of wet blankets on the table, the fire nearly out, and no sign of dinner (and me a school pupil). Of course I'd never put up a fuss— just go along with the rest of my scholarly brothers. Finally the big pot would be put on and an old rubber boot thrown into the stove to get it going. The heaping plate of porridge was good even though it gave me hives, but hell, I had fingernails to scratch, so I bellied up all the porridge I could eat and planned my resting place for the afternoon.

Bill at this time was also a truant and would tell me of his escapades that day. I would pretend I wasn't interested, as though I never went in for that sort of thing. After a few weeks like this, a serious thing happened— six detectives discovered the hideout of the gang of twenty-five (a notorious bunch of hookey players), which was in an old house about a mile from school. They circled the house and got all but two. Billy, called Fox by the gang, was one of the two to escape by jumping two storeys into a dilapidated hen coop. The other guy crawled in an old cellar. Twenty-three were hauled off to jail at 9:30 that unforgettable morning. I was not informed of this until 12:15 by Billy when I came home with the kids I used as my front.

I'll never forget the look on Billy's face at dinner. He was grey with fright; and under the circumstances, I was not so pink myself. Thinking of what Pa would do to him, Billy said seriously that he was going to jump over the cliff, but I cooled him down when I told him I had been on a toot of truancy for nearly two months. Our minds were working overtime to see what we could cook up. It was fifteen minutes to one— no dinner in our stomachs, and you could see we'd aged in a few hours. A quick decision came to me. I said, "Billy, I'm going to school this afternoon. The teacher knows I wasn't among that crowd." I suggested he go Monday morning as the police were looking for him today. With all this talk about jail, police, the teacher, and Pa, it's a wonder I didn't suffer a massive coronary, but no such luck. I took the plunge, leaving Billy to start next morning. Fresh I remember my entrance that afternoon—feeling particularly guilty. But I kept telling myself, "She doesn't have a clue that I was playing hookey."

How I wished my pal, Edward, could have had his mother in his seat. What a duck blind she would have made— about two pick handles across the back, and tall too; but Edward seemed to sink when he sat down and exposed me to the teacher. Seconds after she told the class to be seated, I saw her give me a surprised sarcastic glance. Then she ordered the class to stand. For a second or two I was delighted and still hid behind Edward thinking, "Looks like she's dismissing them for the day. Good Lord, I couldn't be any luckier." Then I saw her jugular veins filling up and she shouted: "Class, meet our visitor." Now all eyes were on me, including girls I was secretly in love with. She continued, "Well, you know he wasn't with those ones who are in jail now. He was all alone playing hookey, but when he found out at dinner time they had been caught, he decided to come to school. Now, class, be seated."

For a few minutes there was whispering, a few laughs, etc., but little did they know the plans my head was considering—should I take off again tomorrow, or maybe right now, as this is a changed place since I left.

Mrs. Brindel began her lesson, which was a continuation of what she had been teaching them before lunch—parsing —analyzing sentences for word, class, sub-class, form, relation, and rule. She must have taught them quite a bit before noon because when she'd poke the pointer at the word and ask, "What goes in the word?", a bunch of hysterical voices would yell, "The word that's going to be parsed." I couldn't make any sense of it because a bunch of altos and sopranos were screeching it out. It was Greek to me. My God, I couldn't stand this mad group, not to mention the teacher. Again, she'd point and ask what went in the word. Finally, after keeping my ear tuned to every scream, I figured I had the answer, as foolish as it seemed. I concluded the class must be saying, "The word that's going to Paris." Now I knew Paris was in France, but why in hell would a word be going there? I began to think they should take the whole damn works to Paris and put them in a crazy home.

Yet, I couldn't help but think how far they were ahead of me, to be learning things like that. I couldn't wait to get out of there, and I asked my friend what time it was (he was fortunate to have his father's watch, no face, guts, or stem, but two good hands). Right then the old buzzard caught me, gave the pointer a good pounding on the blackboard, and yelled to the top of its lungs, "Well, there's our visitor talking when he should be absorbing every minute he can to catch up." The eyes of Texas were on me again. What is she going to ask me? I still hadn't made out what those screeching voices were saying each time she'd nail the blackboard with the pointer.

She told me to stand and I did. I was good at that. Then she took the pointer, pounded it under the word, and said, "What goes in the word?" I thought, "Ah what the hell, I'll take a chance and say that foolish mess the whole class is saying." So I shot right back, "The word that's going to Paris." She turned sort of white, gave me a lovely smile without using her face, and said, "Sit down, Andy, it's a wonder you knew it. Now pay full attention."

She had played right into my hand. If she had asked me "What went in the form?", I'd probably have a dislocated form the rest of my days. Once I'd fathomed what went in the word by listening to the screeches, I figured they were all looney and I didn't want to know what went in the rest if it was as crazy as the first one.

That afternoon was a week to me, with thoughts of Pa and Bill dancing through my head, but I felt I had done a good deed by facing the consequence.

Meanwhile, every cell in the jail was loaded with hookey players, and we were forbidden to talk to the culprits even from a block away. Some were crying for their parents to bring them home, and some never had it so good. They spent a full day in jail and were released after bail. No trial was set but they had to report to the jail every day for a month.

After that long afternoon came the week-end, and people forget a lot in two days. On Monday I was back to my old adventures, alone and watchful.

Young Lochinvar

On one of my rare visits to school, Mrs. Brindel had said the afternoon before, "Now for homework tonight, class, write a composition about the poem 'Young Lochinvar'." The punishment for not doing homework meant a calling down of you, your ancestors, plus ten strappings on each hand. But I never even thought about the poem until ten to nine that ill-fated morning when one of her smart pupils brought up the subject of the composition. My veins clogged, and had I not already been in the school I would have hit for the shore.

23

Every second before nine was precious. In a desperate grab, I got my reader and sat down under an old table in the basement to try my hand at paraphrasing Lochinvar. I was pretty good at writing essays in school, but anything pertaining to a poem left me feeling quite confused. The first two verses went as follows:

Young Lochinvar, came out of the west
Through all the wide borders, his steed was the best.

For a few minutes I tried to figure it out, but then decided it wouldn't make any difference if I'd had five hours as I just couldn't decipher the first two lines. What was a steed? Who was Lochinvar, a Russian or a Canadian? Came out of the west of what— from where? Knowing the bell would ring any time, I had to do something. I did a few ad libs here and there and this is what I came up with:

You know, Young Lochinvar, well, he came out of the west.
From all borders around, his steed was real good.

I continued to write the rest, straight from the horse's mouth almost as it was before my eyes— just switching or adding a few words so as not to lame the sentence. This was done fast and furiously. After finishing all the verses, I still had two minutes before I faced the Fuhrer. I thought that since I had at least made an attempt to tackle it, I was much much safer than those who had done nothing.

Mrs. Brindel looked over the compositions placed on her desk. I knew she'd say something sarcastic and prepared myself for the worst. The class was in one of its quiet moods, me included, when Enemy No. 1 ground out in her rasping voice: "Here's a good composition Andy MacDonald wrote." Then she read it off, not even throwing my extra words in here and there. Then she said, "It's identical to the poem." If I'd had a good lawyer, I could have called her a damn liar.

Anyway it did save me from the gallows— no punishment with the quarter-inch strap— just an extra hour to look at her jib after the smart ones went home. But I had company —about three or four really stupid kids, with both hands swollen so badly from the strapping that they could hardly lift a pencil.

The Day Santa Turned Into a Barn Rat

Drawing was rather hard too. As a matter of fact, I don't remember anything that came easy to me in class except whispering.

At one point I had a sweet lady for a teacher— soft spoken—a smile any time and very interesting to talk to—different from the last one.

It was getting near Christmas and she never worked us too hard, giving us an hour or so to tell tales and relax. This day, she picked up the reader and said, "Class, turn to page one hundred. I want you all to draw this picture and take your time." It was a full page picture of Santa.

It was Friday, 2 p.m., no school tomorrow. I was in a happy mood. Events were running through my head— Pa was going away for the week-end, no lessons, we're having stew for supper, we may get a toilet in the house.

I couldn't wait until I had finished with the physique of old Saint Nick and could go home. I had no conscious interest in him whatsoever. I just kept on adding his features, looking busy like the rest of the kids. The teacher slipped from behind quietly and picked up my drawing of Santa. She said: "Perfect." This surprised me so much that I felt I was going to throw up. She passed it around to all the pupils with an "Ahhhh" from each of them. They weren't surprised so much at it being a beautiful drawing, but that I had finally done something that merited praise.

After it was "Aahhhed" and "Oohhhed" around the room, it came back to the teacher who had a pleasant smile on her face, proud that little 'ole me was her pupil. She placed my drawing in my hand saying, "Andy, take it up to the board and draw it so that the whole class can copy it."

Now this was a clear-cut case of a hero turned dunce. Why, I was there for nearly fifteen minutes and never had so much as a pore drawn. I couldn't make any part of him. Even poor Santa's nice round head was hard to make. It seemed I couldn't draw anything but an oval. I could have finished him faster for the class if the teacher had said, "O.K., Andy, continue making a rat," as I had the drawing of Santa turning into a good-sized barn rat.

What had happened to me? Did I have rat on the brain? How was I going to face the class on my way back to my seat? I know my slick brother Bill would have wriggled out of it. He'd have said it was the chalk.

My seat mate Sid was almost hysterical when I took my seat and that didn't help my situation any. I made him laugh more by whispering to him, "Who drew the damn thing, you or me?" He kidded me for years afterwards about this freak drawing; and for years I've always made it a point not to visit him around Christmas, as his children are still going to school, and there's a possibility they may have me draw the old chap: what he looks like now— and when he was a rat.

The Soup Spoon
The poorer families who lived quite a distance from the school had the privilege of eating lunch at the soup kitchen five times a week. As we got older, Pa, bless his heart, accepted this privilege for us, and that meant we had to go. The only tool required was a spoon; without that you'd hardly be allowed in the large hall, which resembled an army barracks. It was the very low, hungry crowd who went to those free kitchens. Our trip there daily was always done in secret. We had arranged it so that we would head in the direction of home, then cross over and cut through an old bakery yard, knowing that by that time the other boys and girls were well out of sight on their way home.

Arriving at the soup kitchen, we would see about two hundred kids waiting to be fed. The soup was made in big ten-gallon pots. In the centre of the table was the bread and a large can of strawberry jam.

Bill, the gentleman in our house, made it a point to pass up this gobbling party, even though it was against Pa's wishes. As Pa was working in the mines all day, he wouldn't know Bill was home having dinner; and Bill knew we wouldn't squeal on him to Pa. It was to our advantage sometimes, as we would borrow his spoon. He had scientifically devised a place to carry his spoon by sewing two pieces of half-inch-wide elastic garters to the inside of his shirt, which made a firm grip for his spoon but was hard to disentangle when the shirt was thrown in for its weekly wash.

Pa dished out a spoon for each of us, telling us to hold on to it, as it was the only one we were going to get. I don't know whether or not you have ever carried a spoon in your pocket for a week, but it's rather difficult. The spoon he gave me was a blue-silver sugar-shell given to Pa by his grandmother's sister from Scotland, which meant I shouldn't take it around in my pocket, but had to carry it in my hands at all times so that I wouldn't lose it. We had to show Pa our spoon at any given time in the evenings, whenever he called for them. We were always on our guard.

Every precaution was taken not to drop the spoon in school, as a spoon dropping in a classroom, while everyone is drawing, is very noticeable. One day I reached in my back pocket for my handkerchief and with a quick jerk pulled it out, forgetting the spoon was also tied up in it. The sugar-shell landed four desks away from me and danced on the hardwood floor for what seemed like ten minutes before coming to a stop. All eyes left their work to see whence the spoon had come. I played the act so well even my seat mate never dreamed it belonged to me, thank God. The teacher came down, picked up the blue-silver sugar-shell and held it high, asking who had dropped his or her spoon. I was thinking to myself, "I'll not let on, but I'll watch the spoon like a hawk, because I'll have to have it with me when I go home this afternoon."

"Someone must own it," exclaimed the teacher, but I was so absorbed in my drawing I wouldn't look up. She continued, "Whoever owns it will find it on my desk."

My detective mind began to work— I'll wait for a half hour

or so until the pupils' and teacher's minds are off the subject of the spoon and arrange some way to get up to the desk.

Those days we had never heard the word pollution, but I decided to take my scrap paper to the waste basket at the front of the room so that I could get a good peek at the spoon and get it on the rebound. My best chance came with the teacher at the back of the room. Spying the spoon on the left side of the desk on the way up made me feel half safe with Pa. About a foot from the desk I sort of tripped so as to fall on the spoon, which I smothered with my right hand and continued back to my seat. It was done so smoothly, without an eye seeing it, I hardly believed I had it. Acting interested in my drawing, I continued my artwork, with one hand under the desk gripping the spoon I had captured. I decided to put it in my side pocket—then my worries would be over.

Sitting there drawing with a feeling of relief and with only a half hour before school was out, a loud rap came on the door. Feeling happy and mannerly, I sprang from my seat and headed for the door. All eyes of course were focused on my eager frame rushing for the rap. Then, as if tossed with great speed, the spoon slipped out of my unsewn pocket and went hurtling to the floor, bouncing even harder than it had before. Leaving it there on the floor I was only two feet from the door and the class was in titters. How was I going to get out of this one! Here was the same sugar-shell the teacher had placed on her desk a little more than an hour before.

Saved by Gabriel's horn: it was Teedy at the door. He wanted a book that belonged to him. This was my chance. I left the door ajar while I went for the book, and on my way back, when I was directly behind the spoon and even with the door, I gave a hard straight kick while walking and drove my sugar-shell right out into the hall under my brother's feet. Before giving him the book, I whispered a desperate command: "takehomemysugarshell" and slammed the door as fast as I could. A stranger at the door would have rapped again, sugar-shell in hand, but not my brother. He smelled a rat. Everything was perfect now. The teacher was busy giving lessons for the morrow and the noisy sound of a dropped sugar-shell was leaking from their minds.

Arriving home after a day of conniving, I was welcomed by Teedy with my spoon. I made for the thread and needle and took no more chances.

The Pit Mit Stew

On our way home after a long day in school we'd guess what was for supper. Entering the kitchen our facial expressions would show what was cooking. If the herring pot was on, a perturbed look came to the face. But taking up almost two covers on the old stove, the sight of the big pot would bring expressions of pleasure. It meant either soup or corned beef. Generally, herring pots outnumbered stew pots by quite a margin.

Freddy and Pa coming from the mine one frosty evening smiled at the sight of the big pot. Waiting for them to get their heavy coats off, we knew supper was almost ready.

A warming closet on the stove was hidden beneath old socks, odd gloves, and mitts. A wooden bread board covered the stew in the big boiling pot. It took a stout dish cloth for Ma to remove the steam-heated board before she dished out the portions. With that removed the kitchen took on a heavenly aroma.

Dough boys were last to be admitted to the stew, taking a matter of minutes to swell up and cook. While Ma was busily making the "boys", Murray, always ahead of us in his darning, reached for his threadbare sock on the warming closet and unknowingly knocked Freddy's pit mit into the stew.

Capillary action took over immediately, and the weighted mit sunk. Black froth bubbled up from the bottom of the stew and formed on top. Dough boys turned from snow white to slate colour and delicious odours ceased. Everyone was seated, sitting with knives and forks in hand.

Filling the first plate, Ma reached to the bottom with the large two-tined fork to study the curiosity. Neither meat nor vegetables did she have on her fork, but Fred's once black mit, bleached almost white from the boiling stew. Faces dropped. Nothing in the pot could be salvaged, and Ma placed it on the porch floor still steaming.

Suddenly there was the sound of footsteps on the old stone step and the thumping of feet to get rid of snow. The door opened and a not-much-poorer neighbour came in, inquiring about the steaming pot. Ma told her the tale and said she was welcome to the stew such as it was. In a minute the neighbour was off through the snow to her hungry tribe. One hour later the empty pot was returned without a word.

In the meantime we had turned to our old standby, bread and molasses.

Three

Pa's Saving Ways

Always Sexily Attired
Pa, as I said, was very frugal, not only in buying food but also in clothing his family. In Grade One, he bought Murray and me a pair of rubber boots, which were to be kept spotless no matter what the weather. We worshipped those boots and slept with them beside our bed as we loved their rubber smell. But a dry spell set in and we couldn't wear them. Then one hot spring day when Pa wasn't in sight, we wore them to school thinking we'd get home before Pa. Spying an open manhole cover in front of the school, we lowered ourselves into the manhole. What a delightful surprise to discover this test for our boots—until we went right over the tops of them. We sloshed our way home and hid them behind the stove to dry. It didn't take Pa long to find them and he boomed, "Where in the name of God did you find water? Were you in the ocean?" We had to go without them for two weeks, and of course it was at the start of this punishment period that the rains finally came.

Also assigned to us was one pair of sneakers a year, and God help the poor soul who was missing a lace.

Metal protectors were put on all our shoes to ensure their life. I'm sure we were the only people in North America, besides football players, golf pros, and horses, who had iron on our hooves. Our Sunday shoes, which were getting newer each time we wore them, were loaded with them. And thieves would get off with less than Pa's sentence if we lost one protector off these shoes.

How embarrassing it was when Ted would come in to church minutes late with everything really quiet, except for the sound of his feet. If you had taken a horse down the aisle, there would have been just a steady thump, but with Teedy's uneven clicks, Murray, Billy, and I, cuddled and warm next to Pa, knew by the sound of his shoes he was missing two protectors on the left shoe, left side, and one on the right heel — three missing in all. Arriving home, the trial lasted two minutes. We saw the look on Ted's sad face when he lifted his feet as a horse would to be shod. I couldn't stand to wait and hear his sentence. He got a stiff one this time— a lot of people thought Teedy had died. He was out of circulation for the summer months. The first day of school after the summer holidays, he told the teacher he hadn't had his vacation like everyone else. Everybody laughed, but it was no joke with him.

Besides footwear, each of us had one suit a year, used just for Sunday school and church. We had to put them on early Sunday morning, and they had to remain perfect for the rest of the day. In Pa's presence we were as stiff as robots so as not to wrinkle the material.

To hang our suits we were assigned nails with our initials on them. Woe to the one whose pocket flap was inside out or hanging on the wrong initial. Pa would get you. You would wonder why he was dragging you upstairs by the ear. Standing in front of the nails, he would say, "Look at your flap," and just as you'd start to fix it he would give you his famous kick.

Everything had to be perfect when we were dressed up. The lapels had to be outside, boots shined, and the shirt buttoned right. Once I was out to supper with a friend whose father was a good friend of Pa's. When I came home and told Pa where I'd been, all he said was, "Go look at the way your shirt is buttoned." Two extra buttons were resting on the lower part of my chin. At least I had a rest after supper. I ended up in bed for the night.

It seemed no matter how hard we tried to take care of them, something always happened to our clothes; like the twenty-below-zero day in January when Teedy and I went looking for a setting hen. It was a Sunday, and I had on my only suit. I crawled through a fence to this lady's house and ripped the back right out of my suit. Instead of asking for a clucking hen, I had to ask her to sew the suit for me— and move backwards in Pa's presence for a whole year.

My next episode with disaster came one day when I had worn a brand new shirt to school. The fire drill bell rang, and we went down the two flights of stairs and outside. When we came back, the teacher was disgusted with the way the drill went. She said we were to have another drill to make up for the poor one and that we were not to go out like lame cows. I whispered to Murray, "Let's let on there really is a fire and see who gets outside first, you or me?" The fire bell rang. I didn't wait for anything. I was out of my seat, out the door, and down both flights of stairs before she even told the class to line up. As I scrambled to the bottom of the stairs, I could make out a blur standing there with hands on hips. It was the principal. He grabbed me by my new shirt, pulling all the buttons off and tearing the material along with them. Things didn't go well for me that day as I was worried Pa might kill me, but Ma made the principal buy me a new shirt; and after a little mending and ironing, I was the only one in the family with two shirts.

Then there was the time Teedy had trouble with his shirt. Teedy, Murray, Billy, and I were always ready to participate in any sports the town had to offer.

Once the school had a scrub game and picked sides. Murray, Teedy, and I were on one side, while Billy was on the opposing team. Billy's team came tearing down the line, and we charged them. One of the biggest guys on Billy's team made a dive at Teedy and tore his shirt right off. The ball wasn't what we were after then. We knew what a whipping Pa'd give

Teedy when he found the torn shirt. We'd get a good one too just for being accessories to the fact. The three of us waited for this big guy to come down the field with the ball. He lost the ball but we didn't give a damn for it. Instead the three of us jumped on this guy's back— and he had plenty of back to jump on. The surprise really came when one of his own men raced from the opposing pack and jumped him along with the rest of us. It was brother Bill. With the four of us brothers of one mind, we delightedly tore the shirt right off the guy's back. It was the only time Billy played two sides at once.

Another frightening experience was the time Ma bought some stockings at a fire sale for Murray and me. How proud we were to wear those black-ribbed high cotton stockings. Ma presented us with them early one Sunday morning. We had short pants on, and the socks were outstanding on our legs. We had been drilled a thousand times by Pa to take care of our clothes, with the understanding it was the last we were getting. Ten minutes after having them on, Murray called me aside with a look of horror in his eyes. At the top of the heel of his stocking was a large hole. He wanted immediate action from me to remedy the situation. So I went into the house and got a needle and black thread. He and I went down to the shore to mend the trouble.

It was like trying to sew shell ice together. The thread wouldn't hold on either side. The more I sewed, the larger the hole got. It got worse and worse until the hole was almost around the ankle. I said, "Mine are just like new." Then, I took off my shoe to show him and found they were also peppered with holes in the sole that no one could fix. Murray was soothed a little seeing mine. We were due for Sunday school, and so we figured we'd do the best dodging we could around Pa, then go to other authorities, our sisters, and spring the news on them.

On the way up from the shore we were in a hurry, and I ran too close to a guide wire on the hydro pole. A lone broken wire sticking out hooked my good stocking and held every piece of it on the wire, except the sole. It was mangled so badly that sewing, patching, and hiding it was impossible.

Murray went in the house first, on a slant, with the good part of his stockings facing Pa. I waited in the hen barn for the all-clear signal. My only good sock was now tattered with holes the size of quarters, enlarged more by each thumping heartbeat. I kept wishing this was a nightmare I would awake from.

Then Murray opened the door, smiled, and said, "Pa's not home." I was never happier in my life. We both went in and showed Ma. She went into a fit of laughter and said, "I guess you pay for what you get." She told us they had been bought at a fire and smoke sale for ten cents a pair, and she reached down and pulled off the remaining shreds.

One time, Pa, in one of his saving moods, bought me a pair of plus fours. They had a couple of moth holes in them, and so he got them at a bargain price. But who was wearing them in those days? Possibly King George V for fox hunting. Anyway, I had to wear them to church, and I felt out of this world. From behind I looked important, but front to I looked like a curious smulk. They were made for a man size 48, and I only took size 24. The tuck was taken in with a mammoth safety pin, which was my constant worry to keep hidden.

The man who usually took collection wasn't in church, and so it was up to one of us younger ones to take the plate, which was sitting on the floor near my seat. All eyes went to me to pass the plate. I got up like a costumed old English King and walked towards the plate. I realized too late I should never have stooped down for it. I should have had someone pass it to me. But as I bent down, lo and behold the large pin that was the main valve to my golf pants snapped open. Spreading took place instantly. Here I was moving around with the plate, looking like I was wearing a giant's overcoat with my legs through the arms and suspenders holding up the slack. There were about fifty church-goers for me to service with the plate, but my strutting was slowed down to a snail's pace, and I only did half the people. It was all I could do to get back to my seat. My brothers and friends were muffling some good titters, knowing exactly what my troubles were but not coming to my aid. Then came the torture test of stooping to put the plate down again. I had to do it soon as I was about to lose my pants. As I bent down the pin spurred me deeply, and I gave a muffled grunt that was picked up only by my brothers.

Not only were we always handsomely attired— the sexiest time of all was when spring came and Pa, to save money on haircuts, would shave our heads bald, just like a sheep getting a fleecing. If you had a girl in school at that time it was too bad, because by the time Pa finished with his horse clippers, you were scarred quite badly, on top of the baldness.

Teedy, with a round Charlie Brown head, looked like a human pumpkin, with body attached. Whenever we got this shearing, we would be late for school. This meant we had to stand at the door inside the school until the teacher asked why you were late, etc. And if she was in the process of telling the class something, she might let you stand there for twenty minutes.

The kids would take one look and that was it. How could they keep from laughing when the last time they saw you, your head was swarming in curls? We always had an answer to their questions of why we'd gotten it all cut off. "It's so much cooler," we'd answer, although the temperatures at nights ranged in the thirties.

The Sexy Bathers

Pa would never dream of buying us bathing suits— it would have been like asking for a mink coat. So after a hot afternoon of berry picking we'd have a leisurely swim, usually in our inexpensive bare skin.

Swimming with our sisters wasn't much of a worry, as they'd always find an old housedress to hide our virility. There wasn't much chance of drowning in an outfit like that, as we were visible from quite a distance; and when the wind flowed in through the opening at the bottom, it acted like a life preserver. Most dresses handed us were never sized to meet our measurements and if you were a lone swimmer, ten-to-one a rescue plane would fly low to see if you were a flyer tangled up in your parachute.

Bill could only stand so much of those wet dresses, which showed his hidden qualities. So it wasn't long before he came forth with an expensive bathing suit out drying on someone else's line.

He always checked the beach first before wearing it to make sure the owner wasn't around. Then feeling safe, he would come forward like Tarzan to show off his good build. We were more of the Jane type and only applied our dresses on two hundred yards of sandy beach around the rugged jutting of the cliffs, so that we wouldn't be seen.

Those dresses, about a hundred and fifty per cent wool, would take days to dry, because we carried them bundled up in a paper bag, letting other bathers think it was our lunch. Stepping into those dresses on a cool windy day was the same feeling as having a shower outdoors in January.

Sleeves were an awful nuisance, and after a few strokes we found it took a strong man to do the breast stroke using both arms without fatigue.

No matter how wet or dry your costume was, the smell of salt, seaweed, and wool permeated the air— at least the first two should have been good for the lungs.

I don't know if Billy felt sorry for me one sunny day or if he was downright ashamed of me, because looking at my wet figure in profile this day, he said, "I'll have to get you one." I did look pitiful standing there with my bathing dress on inside out and backwards. Bill continued, "Just wait until this evening. I'm going to Greener's Wharf. I know a fellow who swims in the morning, then leaves his suit on the wharf to dry. I'll see you tonight."

Waiting for Bill's return from the theft, I felt terrific. My temperature, blood pressure, and pulse were perfect without a doctor's advice because I was happily envisioning myself in a suit made especially for swimming. Pa or anyone in the family weren't to know a thing about the gift Bill was to present to me. Everything was pointing in my favour. I could see Bill in the distance carrying a brown paper bag. Bill passed me the parcel saying, "The best I could do, under the circumstances." I reached for the moist brown bag. The bag seemed very heavy, and I asked Bill if his suit was in it too. With a negative nod, he told me he was wearing his for underwear, which never surprised me, knowing Bill. Gently, I reached a happy hand into the bag and was dismayed at finding so much material for such a peaked frame.

There weren't too many really big people in Sydney Mines —maybe about two or three that were outstanding; and as far as thinking these big creatures went swimming, it just didn't cross my mind. My figure wasn't robust— about a hundred and ten pounds, a sunken chest, and a weak rear, very noticeable in a wet wool dress. But I was relieved I hadn't discarded my huge dress, as I was a dream in it compared with the tent suit Bill had now grabbed for me in such a hurry. The dimensions of the owner were known by everyone who lived in town.

The owner of this suit weighed close to three hundred and fifty pounds and stood a massive six-foot-three. Holding the suit in front of me for size, it was so large that I was completely hidden from view.

The colour was a beautiful deep blue (my favourite colour) with blazing red bands running around both legs; but good Lord, it would almost go around our small post office.

"Take it in," Bill said, but I had my doubts about there being a seamstress or sewing machine in Canada that could alter it to my fit. It was good for nothing, and so we went to the fellow's house, rapped innocently at his door, and asked him if he had lost his tights. A wide happy grin enveloped his huge head, thinking what honest kids we were— and me with the words almost falling off my tongue that his trunks were way too large.

Back home with night drawing nigh, I sighed deeply and opened my bag. I hung my house dress on the line so that I could start out with a dry warm feeling next day when the winds were high and the sea choppy. Sometimes on days like that I wouldn't even get ducked, knowing that the suit would cling to my shivering body for weeks without drying if I dared make the plunge. I'd be so warm and comfortable in that mass of wool, I would just jump from rock to rock, the dress fluttering in the breeze, looking like a befuddled eighteenth century actress.

The Crows

Pa also gave us a lot of trouble in the mitten area. We were given only one pair of mitts on the first of winter. They had small thumb stalls even before they were used. Why they hadn't made the thumb extra large puzzled us. Pa's orders were that we weren't to throw snowballs as it would soak the mitts, causing shrinkage.

We never made snowballs in Pa's presence, but as soon as there was a house or tall fence to obstruct his view, the bending and making started. We had to place our mitts on the warming closet of the old coal stove at day's end so that they'd be ready for the morning tramp to school. They were in full view for Pa's scrutiny. After the first good day of throwing, mine began to shrink. You never saw such a reduction of wool in so short a time. First my thumb closed entirely, but that wasn't much of a problem as I'd throw my thumb in with the four fingers. My worry was when I put them on the warming closet with the rest of the mitts. You'd see the drastic results beside those of my brothers, who hadn't yielded to temptation that day.

With theirs new and mine in desperate shape, my brothers did everything to help me survive Pa seeing them under the others, but Fate took over one evening. Murray had decided to get another armful of wood in Pa's presence, giving Pa a sample of how good he really was— always thinking of home and hearth. I was caught off guard and didn't notice Murray doing his good deed. My withered mitts were under Murray's for protection and were now in full view to Pa— they looked like a small mouse without legs cuddled up in a ball. Pa picked them up with a look as if to say, "Should these be here?" What could I say? (Excuses were getting scarce after all the other acts of disobedience we had committed.) I told the lie, backed up by my brothers, that even when they were new they were too small and that even my small-handed brother couldn't get them on. When no colour came to Pa's face, the worry of punishment wobbled out of my mind.

The next morning was fiercely cold, and Pa decided I should wear his mitts, which he could do without as they were the mitts he wore under his leather ones. Those he gave me were very,very large: from tip to wrist about a foot and a half long, about six inches across, and black as tar. The thumb stall alone was as big as the finger stalls in mine, so shrinkage wasn't a problem for a change.

These being Pa's mitts, I never had to be warned of the care I should take of them. They looked like crows and it wasn't minutes after receiving them they were christened "the crows". But wanting to make them exactly like crows, I slipped to the hen-house when Pa left for work and plucked two black tail-feathers from a hen, who didn't appreciate it a bit. I sewed the feathers lightly on each end of the mitt, using the thumb for the head. It was an exact duplicate of a crow, so good that I made another trip to the hen-house to get some more material to complete my pair. I noticed the hen I had plucked before was keeping a head-on look at me, avoiding every angle that might give me access to her tail. The big black rooster was strutting around, not only with a chip on his shoulder, but also with an abundance of glamorous black feathers on his tail. I made my thrust and came up with a few extras. Dressing those crows up the next morning was my delight.

Wearing them to school was one laughing pleasure for me and my brothers. The mitts came to my shoulder blades and were secured by a lace at the wrist. Trying to avoid the kids seeing them, especially girls, I released the lace, with the help of one of my brothers, about a block from school. The mittens kept my hands red hot, and so I could eliminate the thought that they would ever get cold from there to the school.

I stuffed them down my pant leg, with no fear they'd fall

out, as the openings of the pant legs were muffled by the woollen socks pulled up over the pant cuffs and rolled down comfortably over the gum rubber tops. (Why, you could almost smuggle a brother into the show as our pants were always bought large to allow for nature and shrinkage from washing in P & G soap.)

I wasn't long in school when ideas came to my head ... that long, long period from 2 p.m. until 3:30 p.m. seemed to take days to pass ... then the teacher decided to leave the room, after giving us some work to concentrate on and the old command not to talk. She wasn't three seconds over the threshold when I reached down and pulled up one of my crows. Holding it in a flying position, I came up with a fierce caw, and the class went hysterical. Everyone thought I had captured a real crow. Murray was the only one who knew and kept edging me on to take the other crow out, but I didn't dare because the noise in the room was getting uncontrollable and I was too worried about calming down fifty-five pupils before the teacher returned.

Shoving the mitt down my pant leg just minutes before the teacher arrived saved the day and me. An odd snicker here and there were dealt with by the teacher with no blame attached to me. She never found out why the class was so bright and jolly-looking when she came back, and I was relieved to have such sincere classmates. The afternoon passed much faster now; it was no time before we were lined up for the long trek home.

Murray could run much faster than I. If there was a horse and sled going fifty miles an hour a hundred yards ahead of him, he'd end up catching it and would stand on the runner.

On our way home, Murray began running after a sled. I was in hot pursuit behind him, mitts and all reaching out for Murray's out-stretched hand. But instead of pulling me onto the sled, he pulled the crow off my hand. Slacking up on my useless mission, I slowed down to a lope. About a mile down the road there was Murray waiting for me— with no mitt. He had lost it in the little old man's sled.

41

This man lived miles from our place, and so the hunt was on for the mitt. With one hand extremely warm and the other barely usable, we headed in the old man's direction. Two miles on foot later, we finally came to his house. Being as fiery as his horses, he already had them undressed and munching on their oats.

Strange dogs never accepted Murray's attire at any time, and our worry as we entered the gate was, "Has he a dog?" At the gate and thirty or so feet from the house, I made a dash for a door in the small back porch. Suddenly out came a huge mad dog with nothing on its mind, I figured, but to get me first, then use my twin for dessert. While the dog came after me with terrific speed, Murray was nowhere in sight.

I had one mitt left with the feathers, and at one turn in the yard I flew up a leafless tree. After I landed, my mitt fell to the ground, a dark contrast on the white snow. The mad dog smelled around the feathers and mitt giving me ample time to climb higher. I just knew Murray would be home by now. The dog's snarling and barking soon had the small old man out in the yard.

Seeing the black mitt on the snow before he saw little white me on the tree, the old man looked puzzled. Turning his head without moving his body he looked me square in the eye: "What are you doing and where did you come from?"

This relieved me from some of the thumping going on inside my sweater. I couldn't tell him fast enough. "Will the dog bite?"

"All depends; what do you want?"

Well, I told him my story and I can't say I saw tears of sympathy in his eyes. He put the dog in the house before I got to ground level with him. I picked up my crow. To the barn we went, his wife peering out from a breath-cleared patch of frosted window, thinking I was a cattle buyer. The old man reached under a few empty potato bags, having sold them house to house that day, and came up with the other crow. With a better feeling now, I marched the road home.

Pa was held up at the mine, owing to some trouble with the

man-car that took them from the mouth of the mine to town. I had just lifted two frozen feet over the kitchen threshold when Pa crossed five minutes later. Plenty of vacancies on the old warming closet: I took the feathers off my crows and laid them out side by side.

Milder weather soon dispelled my worries, and Pa took his mitts back. I never threw out my original small ones, which by now looked like two-inch cuffs. I was much happier, as I felt I had my own belongings, and I did my best through the years not to get any help from Pa's clothing.

The Tasty Fig

Pa, to conserve his energy, was always getting us to run his errands for him. If he had done them himself, he would have fared a lot better, and so would have we.

A pipe or cigarette smoker wasn't allowed to smoke down the mine, and so most miners chewed tobacco. Pa was one of them. He was a fussy chewer.

MacDonald's Twist was his favourite. It was about six inches long, a half-inch wide, and a half-inch thick. Some of the figs were a red colour, dry and not juicy. The others were black and juicy. Pa would want the black, juicy kind. If we ventured home with a red dry one, he'd analyze it, see it wasn't a black, juicy fig, and send us right back to the store, which was over a mile away, to exchange it.

How we hated this exchange errand, but the red dry one gave Pa the heartburn and this he wouldn't chance. The figs came in boxes, like loose dates. You would usually find some good storekeeper who would gladly exchange it. They would let you go to the box, which held nearly a hundred, and pick your choice.

Sometimes you would find a nice, black, juicy one in the centre; then you'd know you had it made. But most of them were dry through and through. The other miners were always satisfied with whatever they grabbed, but not our Pa. Usually by the time he had analyzed the fig we had brought him, the store would be closed.

One evening Murray came home with a blood-red, dry fig. He showed it to us before he gave it to Pa— it was one of the worst we had ever seen. We worried Murray so badly that he came up with a plan. He took black boot polish and applied it to the fig, then put some molasses between the layers.

He presented the fig to Pa who smiled when he saw it. Murray was promptly appointed the only one he would trust to get the best in figs. We knew the secret and were delighted that Murray was picked number one man, leaving us out of a mission we had fouled up many a time by bringing on Pa's heartburn. Not only was he elected to buy Pa's chewing, but also, after a few of Pa's buddies chewed a chaw of Pa's fig, they got Murray to buy black, juicy, fresh figs for them too.

The Floating Blueberries

We never seemed able to carry out Pa's orders properly, even when it came to picking blueberries.

August, the blueberry-picking month, was now upon us, and Pa, figuring Murray and I had too much idle time on our hands, came home from a neighbour's one evening with the news that there was a boat taking pickers across the harbour to Low Point (some three miles). The fee per picker was twenty-five cents, and Pa had volunteered the both of us to go.

We knew the dory we were to go in, many times having nearly drowned while rowing it around the shores. Pa was ignorant of this plus the fact the dory was christened *The Coffin*. It was one thing skimming around the shores in it, but to make the full three-mile trip across would be like going to the moon.

When Pa gave us the fifty cents for the journey, we knew that was it— we had to go; and we both dreamed we drowned that night. When we weren't dreaming of drowning, we were both sitting up in bed looking at each other, thinking of the trip and the watery graves that awaited us.

At seven o'clock next morning, we went down to the shore where the other pickers, with enough containers to hold one hundred watermelons, were gathered. The owner of *The Coffin*, a man with a vile tongue who wasn't liked by anyone, and his two sons, who were much like him, were there, along with his wife, a thin, sickly woman, who was counting her blueberry utensils. She was a sweet old lady who, because of her Newfoundland heritage, loved the water and wouldn't have objected to a trip across by inner tube. In her early seventies, she made Murray and me feel quite aware of our cowardice.

It was always calm that early in the morning and so the trip over was nice, but as we neared the other side, the swells were beginning to start.

We were taught to respect our elders, but not in emergencies. When we got to shore, Murray and I crawled over the old lady, nearly tossing her into the water, just to get our footing on the almighty land. The boat was pulled up by the men and tied to a stake. The pickers got out, their containers rattling like a jazz band. Up the cliff to the picking grounds we went and then the grabbing began. The berries hung like grapes. Murray would come to me every ten berries and tell me to look across the water. What a sick feeling we had when we saw those huge white caps, which had suddenly turned up with a fifteen-mile-an-hour breeze.

The rest were greedily picking berries with both hands at a terrific rate of speed, with no thoughts of the angry waters we'd have to face hours later. How could we pick berries and watch every turn of the wind and tide at the same time? Someone had to worry, and so we worried for them all.

The old lady must have picked a hundred pounds to our five-pound molasses can. She didn't look up for hours, but scooped across the plain like an earth mover grabbing everything blue with both hands. Murray came again to tell me that one breaker was as big as a gasoline boat— and us with a leaky dory and a wired-up oar. I think we ran small fevers.

I noticed Murray edging towards the men to pick, as they had a good spot, and I hung around with the old lady, not keeping up to her but just picking. Everything was quiet. Pickers never talk when berries are plentiful.

All of a sudden in between peeks at the ocean, something happened that had never happened before. I was savagely stung by a bee on top of the head. It was as if a person had driven a narrow sharp nail four inches long right through the top of my head. Never having experienced such pain before, I had no thought of bees. I thought the terrific sudden stab had come from a human being and that being would have to be the old lady, the only one close to me in any direction.

Knocking my berry can over, I raced towards the old lady, who I figured must be insane to have pulled such a stunt. All I could see was her back, with her hands still fleecing in the berries. I ran up to her, screaming hysterically, "What did you stick in my head?" When she saw the anguished look on my face, she stopped picking. Up she jumped throwing her long straight grey hair back over her shoulders and tried to figure me out. I was holding my head as the pain was intense. After saying, "Son, let me see," she diagnosed my wound as a bee sting and rushed to the shore for some damp mud to poultice it.

A bee sting like that didn't help me fill my bucket as I had something else to worry about now besides the swells and white caps. I now watched and shooed away from me anything that flapped or flew. Murray arrived with his can full, and after telling him about my mishap, he helped me fill my can to the brim.

The men were now walking down to the boat and placing their cans, bottles, slop pails, and dish pans on the floor of the leaky carrier. The old lady came over the hill with her grab, possibly a hundred pounds, carrying both containers, one under each arm, with a winning smile on her wrinkled face.

This was the time to eat, so everyone got their little brown, wrinkled bags out. Of course Murray and I had made love to our lunch minutes after landing ashore, and so we were quite hungry watching them eat almost the same kind of sandwiches as we had had, except with a little less molasses.

The men tried to look and act tough, knowing Murray and I were scared to death to even think of leaving dry land for the trip back. After those characters ate, they folded up their brown bags, tucked them in a dirty pocket, and positions were taken in the boat. Before loading, Murray and I had a secret meeting, trying to figure out the safest part of *The Coffin*. Which part would sink last? We came to a final agreement that the front end would go down first, and so we were to hang back until everyone was aboard. We two huddled down in the back of the boat like Siamese twins, clutching our cans in one hand and a death grip on the side of the boat with the other. The rolls and white caps were huge, and the wind was much stronger by now. The old lady was up front as though daring to be drowned. The two sons were on the oars with the father bailing out ankle-deep water, and we were only thirty feet out. Waves would break near the boat, a salt spray covered us and our berries, and the sea never lessened its boiling. It appeared to us that there were too many in the boat, along with the berries. The nose of the boat was never straight. It had about a seventy-degree angle, and a breaker could have overturned the whole thing. Changing the oars was our biggest worry. We knew the father would have to have a crack at the rowing, just to show us what a seafaring man he was.

When one of the sons changed with the father, a huge wave came and almost swamped the boat. Every blueberry was floating in the water, and it was a job to hold on to our cans.

Only a half mile out and looking ahead, there seemed to be no end. As much as we respected the old lady, if they had figured there were too many in the boat, we would have suggested throwing her overboard. They kept the boat from going side on and told their mother to go aft. She knew right away what to do, but Murray and I, not knowing the language of sailors, wondered where she would go, especially in this small boat. She trickled her way back towards us and for a moment we thought she was going to keep right on going past us over the side, and we weren't making any attempt to save her, not even loosening our grip, being kind of glad to get rid of her. We had both hands clutching the sides of the boat now, as cans, berries and all, were in the bottom of the boat.

She cuddled beside us like a huge caterpillar waiting for its wings and with a calm smile on her face, as though she were sitting on a crowded bus on dry land. The father looked at us and said, "Now you bies go bow," so we bowed graciously, thinking this was his order. He pointed towards the front, and so we willingly floated through the air to the front. After being there for ten rough minutes, he gave another screech, "Go stern!" Both of us, awaiting his every command, stiffened out only to be beckoned to the back of the boat again by the old lady.

So back we went, thinking there's discrimination even in a boat. The back must sink first, so that's the reason we were ordered to the back. To our minds, the old woman should get out now and make it easier for us to survive. We were still young. She'd lived her life. We clung and prayed as we kept looking at miles of water ahead, churning like wet carbide.

It took an hour to row across to pick the berries. We had spent three hours already going back, and we were only half way. The little old woman had opened some gum, and I was thinking, "Look, no hands, she's not even holding on." Murray and I were praying she wouldn't offer us any, as our hands were gripping each side of the boat.

Finally the other shore was sighted, and we turned our heads in that direction, marvelling at the sight of land again. Our hearts and nerves were beginning to register now. We were whimpering to each other again. As we got nearer, our voices got stronger and our grip lighter. But now the loss of the berries was beginning to bother us. We tried to salvage a few salt-sprayed ones from the bottom of the boat, but most of them were squashed. Our minds were coming slowly back to normal, and we wondered if they would give us back our fifty cents. The shore was about three hundred feet away now, and there was a crowd forming on the shore, wondering and shocked to see us alive.

Telling Pa our adventure, he felt rather guilty about having forced us to go. Next morning we went down to the flats

ninety feet from our house and picked enough for three blueberry pies.

Four

Christmas Capers

1 Duck— 2 lb.
11 children— 1500 lb.
Ma and Pa— 300 lb.
Total Ma and Pa and kids = 1800 lb.
Amount of duck each consumed— 1/555 lb. and still hungry.

Oh, My Poor Duck
That feeling of Christmas for a child is one he'll never have again. Just to hear the word "Christmas" spoken was a thrill, even in July.

A week before Christmas we were at our best, willing to do anything for any member of the family without argument. A few days before Christmas, Pa would give each of us a dollar bill to buy something for ourselves. How we appreciated that! What great affection we had for Pa who had been so rough on us throughout the year.

Billy was the slickest of us all. He would always buy Pa a good substantial present, not with thoughts of love, but speculating on a gift from Pa that would cost much more than his. With the Christmas spirit spreading over us, we'd go to town next day to look over the toys.

Our scheme was to buy as many gifts as a dollar could buy,

without taking too much of the dollar. I bought a metal duck with a winder on it. When wound the duck would flap and quack. It cost sixty-nine cents, but for the first few days it was priceless. As soon as I'd open my eyes in the morning, the duck would be on my mind. I guess I thought too much of it. The greatness of it couldn't go on forever. One morning Teedy walked on it with a pair of heavy shoes and cut off all circulation to the quack and the flap. We tried everything to repair it. I can still see the look on the duck's face, as though it were suffering pains and aches in its crushed tin body.

But Teedy had a frog, which croaked and jumped when you wound it. Nowadays, in retaliation, a brother might jump on the frog and behead it, but that never crossed my mind. I just wanted half-interest in the frog in return for the damage inflicted on my duck. Since the duck was ground-born for good, all my attentions went to the frog. It was constantly on my mind. Teedy then issued a bulletin that he would wind him twice to my once. I accepted this, and things were going wonderfully for a few days. Then one mild day in January when Teedy was nowhere in sight and snow was scarce, I figured the frog would do better outside in the wide open spaces. So I took Mr. Frog outside for his first outdoor show. I'd wind him up and watch him croak and leap. I was so interested in this marvellous frog, I forgot about eating. I devoured all his actions instead. I was thinking about my good fortune in having this frog all to myself outdoors when I saw the coal man coming with his horse and cart. I had to open the gate for him and his horse.

Seeing a horse was a real novelty; I forgot all about the frog and concentrated on the live horse, watching the way he knew where to go and what to do automatically. The coal was dumped and the horse took his round-about course to turn. I watched, spellbound by the sight of his muscular rump, while those big cart wheels, spoke by spoke, went over Teedy's frog. In seconds that shapely frog was completely round. The shock was tremendous. It was so severe that I forgot to shut the gate. I kept wondering, "What can I do to make it look like a frog?" But nothing I could do would help its condition. Soon Teedy arrived on the scene and when I presented him with the round frog, he went into a state of shock, not realizing I was just coming out of one. He cried and cried while I frantically tried to form a frog or anything out of the shambles I had adopted half of.

Eventually our sorrow spent itself, and we pooled the remainder of our dollars. We had eighty-two cents between us to shop with. That was big money in those days. Then we got a terrific idea. We decided to buy a live rabbit; in fact, the man who sold them gave us two for our money and said to take good care of them like he did. He couldn't have given them to better owners. We would have breathed for them if that were possible. Home we came with the rabbits, anxious to make them a perfect home. The white one was to be Teedy's and the brown and white one mine. Sleep meant nothing to us. We had live creatures to take care of. They ate much better than us for a while. Not having much time to make them a home before dark, we took them to an old hen-house and fixed up a temporary place for them. Ted's white rabbit was a lovely sight to see. Even to me it was the head of the party, and so we gave it the best place in the hen barn. I arranged a place for mine up over a few boards, which would do until the morning when we could make a better place.

Early next morning Ted and I went out to see our lovables. I found my brown rabbit stretched out full length. A board had fallen during the night and struck him squarely on the head. This was a rabbit punch that would have been fatal to any rabbit. Ted's rabbit was in paradise, while a calamity had fallen upon mine. We gave him a burial Pope Paul would have received. We prayed at his funeral, placed him in a box, and marched him to a special place in the garden. Ashes to ashes and dust to dust were sprinkled, and the lid softly closed over him.

We didn't mourn the rabbit's death for as long as we normally would have because we had Christmas to look forward to.

I'm Jack Spratt, But She's Too Fat

In school the Christmas tree concert was a great event. A tree was mounted and colourfully decorated. At school we appeared happy and joyous, but at home calm and collected, owing to the fact that Pa was never affected by this good cheer until a couple of days before Christmas.

I was unfortunate enough to have Mrs. Brindel for three different grades; and while the teachers with love for the Yuletide were lining things up for their party with recitations and transferring pretty pictures of reindeer on to the blackboard two weeks before Christmas, Mrs. Brindel was telling us to take out our geography book. This to us was like smoking around a gasoline pump.

When the door was open and the room drowned with Christmas songs from the other classrooms, she'd slam the door hard as if to say "Humbug! Let's get on with our work." She would have been the ideal teacher for Grade One and Two to explain to the five- and six-year-olds why there was no Santa Claus. She might even have gotten out a chuckle.

A few days before Christmas she'd let her hair down and start rushing out a few plays here and there, but even this never made us like her any better. She'd never want any of us to laugh or to catch her laughing.

I was never the type to be picked for a play— only playing behind the scenes, like thumbing my nose at her when her back was turned.

But somehow this one year I ended up with a recitation from the old goat a few days before Christmas— not knowing who my partner was until the last minute. Hardly time to memorize my loving part, I was fortunate enough to have heard it about a thousand times from nursery rhymes out of the only book of rhymes we had, passed down from four generations. It was the old story of "I'm Jack Spratt, I can eat no fat, my wife can eat no lean, but between us both, on Christmas Eve, we lick the platter clean."

There I was the day of the play sitting with my empty platter, all aired up to shout my piece, when I turned to see this

53

large creature coming from behind me, floor creaking. I held off my recitation, waiting for this ungodly heavy person to be seated or continue out the door. Instead she threw her large parts up next to me and gave me a sort of "Hi!" look.

Here I was with an empty platter, sitting across from the fattest, homeliest girl in the school with me doing all the talking as she had no part to say—just sit there with her fat body and a stupid look on her face. I even kind of edged away as if she didn't belong there.

"Why hadn't the teacher told me I was to have her as my wife?" Surely, seeing the same kids every day for a full term, the teacher must have had some knowledge of who liked who insofar as flirting was concerned. Why then did she match me up with a character three times my size, knowing full well she'd be the last person I'd have an interest in?

Nervously, loudly, and swiftly I recited my part, then flew to my seat amid thunderous applause, which must have been for her as she was still sitting there.

At those concerts, parents would circle the desks in chairs to hear what their sweet little girls and boys were saying as each recited a small verse. Some kid tensely waiting to perform would walk urgently to the centre of the floor, only to find out he had suffered brain damage on the way and had forgotten every line of his verse—all eyes focused on him. With head dropping just a little towards the floor and a quick sixty-degree sway, a tremendous cry would fill the room, ending in dry sobs. Sometimes these sobs stuck around as long as two hours after you had had a healthy cry. Clapping never helped the situation, as the kid would think, "Hell I never said anything yet and I don't want pity." Had I not gone through this I wouldn't know how to explain it. Why, I was raving and raging for a week or so, showing how I was to come out in front of those spectators.

But when the crucial moment arrived, all motors stopped; my sobs appeared and stayed around even a week after the outburst.

At those Christmas parties, some big shot's daughter would

say her piece so low in volume that even if you had had your ear clamped to her mouth you wouldn't have known what she had said, but the applause she'd get would almost blow her off the stage. Up I'd go, knocking pencils and papers off the desks I passed, with my large jacket open and swinging, heading for that certain spot on the floor where the first thing to be noticed by the multitude was my attire. Not caring for the eyes analysing me, I'd say my piece at the top of my lungs, sometimes roping it out so fast and loud there would be spit accompanying it landing on my chin.

Steering clear of those Christmas plays became my objective. "Mary or Jane can play that part better than me." Besides, what if Pa came to see it; why I'd frizzle up like a lizard when you put salt on him, if I were to say my part and look up to see Pa smiling. Either he or the crowd would get an object thrown at them.

Who Can That Be Under the Robe?
Christmas in church was mostly for the rich. The reason we went wasn't the interest we had or the good it would do us, but to get the small bag of candy and apple which was presented to all. The poor crowd was never in the plays.

I know that if it hadn't been so noticeable and caused such confusion, we would have been rejected in the area of the candy and the apple also. What would happen when we came to these concerts with our buddies trying to cope with those VIPs? We would end up happier than any of the big shots' sons or daughters.

The show would open with a local girl with no desire to even smile at anyone in our class. Out she would come with some wooden pins and juggle them in a scientific way. Her mom and dad would naturally have the closest seat to the stage so that they could drink in their daughter's fantastic talent. The mother and father were on our black list and underlined, the same two having had police after us in school for picking up a few frozen apples from under an apple tree in November.

This juggling was getting monotonous for us as we had also seen her perform in Sunday school and in day school.

We were always willing to laugh at anything that cropped up in the minds of our friends just bubbling with fun. A nativity play and song would always be on the agenda. We'd seen this so much we could have played it ourselves without a teacher.

The stage grew dark and silence reigned. A very dim blue light shone on the shepherd, whom we suspected was a character named John and whose features in reality resembled a toad. We still weren't sure who the "lighted" wiseman was until a brighter light came on and we saw for certain it was John, with a long white robe, walking easily to the child in the manger to the tune of "We Three Kings of Orient Are". It wasn't long before I composed lyrics applicable to John's features, by singing to my buddies in a low whisper:

Who can that be under the robe?
Is it John or is it a toad?
Lift the robe and you will see
If it's John or a T-O-A-D.

This of course, was sung to the tune of "We Three Kings".

Bob Skates Aren't For Swimming

Weeks before the time for the stockings to be hung, when Ma and Pa were visiting neighbours, we could read each others' minds. With Ma and Pa only a few feet out the door, Bill would take us to the hiding place under an unused darkened cupboard. We didn't go there too often as we were told it was a rat hideout and we could get a nasty bite in the dark. As we got older Bill got the nerve to check.

This one Christmas Eve, four pair of bobskates were found. There was a large pond a hundred feet from the house, an ideal place to try them. We forgot that it had been unseasonably mild for the last few days; before us lay four pair of skates. At 2 a.m. with the house in silence, we slithered out of bed like baby snakes. Almost walking on air so as not to make too much noise when our weight hit the twelfth step and it creaked, downstairs we crept. We spied our skates again, which were now sitting under our stockings, which hung on three-inch nails so that Santa could leave each of us one hundred pounds of his loot. (A claw hammer was placed near by to pull out the nails as soon as the stockings were taken down in case Pa might brush up against them, tear off half his shirt, and ruin our Christmas.)

The skates were put on in silence. Led by Bill, we raced to the pond. Though the morning was dark we found the small path, and with a formidable thrust we all followed Bill out onto the darkened pond. The ice, about one thousandths of an inch thick, wouldn't have held a beam of light— yet here we were following Bill at breakneck speed across the pond, waist deep, half crying and half laughing until we reached the other side, a distance of two hundred feet. Taking the skates off, we tried to dry them with our shirt tails. Then, skates over our shoulders and sock-footed, we took the land way home. There, more drying was administered in silence. The skates were placed back under our socks and off we slunk to bed.

Feeling too damp to sleep we whispered until 8 a.m. Then we heard heavy footsteps and we knew Pa was in motion. Like sweetly-behaved kids, we followed him downstairs trying to make a scene of gleeful surprise as in the old English plays. Luckily Pa fell for our act and advised us how we were to take care of our skates by drying them off thoroughly after use, not knowing we had baptized them six hours before in the pond.

The Expanding Pipe
It seemed we were always getting into some kind of deviltry on Christmas eve.

Every Christmas Ma would get Pa an expensive yellow-bowled pipe. She ordered it two weeks before Christmas, and it always got there for Christmas Eve. We knew this pipe was prized by Pa and were extra careful when we saw it on the mantle piece.

It was Ma's custom to give Pa his twenty-dollar pipe on Christmas Eve, and he would always smoke the new pipe that night before he went to bed.

This particular Christmas Eve, Murray and I were looking in the window around 8 p.m., watching Pa smoke his pipe as he talked to Ma who was knitting next to the fireplace.

Our plans were to wait for Pa to go to bed. Then when we got in the house we'd be free to have a smoke. Our smoke would curl and entwine with the smoke left behind by Pa, so if by chance he came downstairs he'd never dream that Murray was using one pipe and that I was trying out his new one.

We went into the front room where Pa's new pipe was still lit. Murray went to the bookcase and from ten old pipes picked his favourite while I was mastering the new one. Pa would leave his pouch filled with tobacco lying next to his pipe. Allowing plenty of time for Pa to retire, Murray came with the long wooden matches— and propping ourselves in chairs, like the Hunchback of Notre Dame, we were all set. Being near the fireplace, the draft from the open fire would draw the smoke up the chimney. Murray lit a long wooden match and passed it to me to light my expensive pipe. As he passed me the light, always playing tricks, he sneakily reached with his other hand and pulled a hair on my arm holding the pipe. Thinking I had been burned, I jerked my arm away, tossing the rich pipe into the hot coal cinders. Reaching into the coals I came up with two parts of the pipe in a hot hand.

Murray's eyes were bulging out of his head as he knew he was to blame, and so our smoking party ended abruptly. We had to come up with a pretty good excuse to cover the serious crime we had committed. With our heads together a solution was soon found. We'd put the pipe back intact exactly as we had found it and say nothing to anyone, not even to Ma.

After breakfast Christmas morning Pa went to the front room, sat in his favourite chair, and reached for his new pipe to have his usual comforting smoke. Calling for Ma we knew exactly what had happened. Murray and I were like the three monkeys see no evil, hear no evil, speak no evil, and we stuck to our guns.

Hearing the discussion between Pa and Ma, we could scarcely believe our ears. Pa said he had only smoked it once and laid it on the table while it was still hot, so the cool table could have caused a quick expansion and snapped the pipe. Ma agreed with him. We were overjoyed with their conclusion and spent a happy Christmas Day.

Returning the pipe to the store after Christmas, the owner put up no argument, replacing it with another yellow bowl, which I wasn't too quick to try out again.

This Cardboard Duck is Delicious
It seemed that we didn't get enough to eat even on Christmas Day. One Christmas morning, Murray and I got an orange cardboard duck each from Santa. They had picked up a beautiful Christmas smell from the oranges in the bottom of our socks. Taking our ducks with us out to the old vacant henhouse, we smelled them every step of the way. We were determined that if the smell continued, there was nothing else to do but eat them and satisfy the craving for the smell that almost drove us wild.

Murray went at his first, starting from the head. Then I decapitated mine, and it took us twenty minutes before our toy cardboard ducks were devoured, with us savouring every morsel. It took a lot of saliva to chew up this pasteboard, but that didn't bother us as that beautiful smell lingered on even when the ducks were in our stomachs.

Now that everything edible was gone, all we had to look forward to was the same boring routine of school again.

What a let-down it was to come back to school— books and pencils in the same position you had left them before Christmas. Teachers had a different attitude towards life. Last time they were bubbling with love. Now it was the "Well, we've wasted a lot of time" kind of Scrooge attitude. I thought this wasn't right and began planning my hookey. If only the teacher had sighed after Christmas and said, "Well, darn, we

have six months of school left, and I hate it as much as you."
Then I might have stuck it out. But she let us know in no uncertain terms she was going to be tough— no more time to waste. I was wondering why I should put in another day of this outright nonsense.

Why should I care if sisal hemp came from the town of Sisal? I could do without sisal. Who needed wool from Argentina? All Pa had to do was go to the store and there was wool right there. Ninety-eight cents for a sweater, which if caught in the rain would require a major operation to remove.

This terrible let-down after Christmas and New Year's still haunts me today. Excitement, love, and everything that goes with it would come to a very abrupt halt.

Our tree was never taken down until nearly the middle of January, its spruce needles quite thin after being in a hot room since December 1. Ten-year-old strung popcorn would be taken off the tree and put away for the next Christmas. During hungry spells, we'd sneak up to the attic and eat the aged pop corn.

Five

The Few Times We Weren't Sick, We Were Accident-Prone

Acute Asphyxiation, Aged Nine

I never seemed to get enough to eat. So one day when I had saved up fifteen cents, I sneaked across to a little store run by an elderly lady. She had a bell wired from her store to her house to signal her when someone was in the store.

On this secret mission to get food the bell seemed to ring even louder, giving away the reason for my early morning visit to the store. It might bring hungry brothers or some poor friends, and then my greedy feast would be over.

The fifteen-cent box of Shredded Wheat with the beautiful picture of Niagara Falls on it was passed to me by the wrinkled old woman. Poking the large box under my small blue sweater and tying the bottom of my sweater with a piece of string, I took the long way home to be free of other hungry mouths.

Down the road I saw a band of my friends coming. They would be curious about my peculiar square chest, and so I hit for the shores. The tide was at its peak and the waves were washing the cliffs with their frothy tongues. My problem was to get around the edge of the cliffs without wetting my package. One time I was up to my waist holding it high over my head. Not caring about the drenching I was getting or the danger of being swept out to sea, I plunged on until I came to a cleft in the cliff. Safe now from prying eyes, I gathered a few dry sticks and started a small fire to dry me out some before starting home. I was soon steaming like dry ice in water. I tried to eat one of the lobster-trap-shaped biscuits, but without milk and sugar it wasn't too palatable. Soon I made my way up the seventy-five-foot cliff to the big field at the top and ran the short distance home, hoping everyone was still asleep so that I could satisfy my craving for the shredded wheat with milk and sugar.

Everything was quiet as I tiptoed in through the porch to the kitchen. Putting two shredded wheat in the bowl and doctoring them up good with lots of milk and sugar, I began to enjoy my longed-for cereal. Greedily I placed a third and fourth one in my bowl.

Then breathing a deep guilty sigh, I clutched at my throat. On my guilty inhalation, I had drawn one of those straw-like fibres into my windpipe. My breathing cut in half and my chest racked with pain, I managed to get out a few weak peeps that were heard by no one but me. After all the trouble I had taken to feast alone, I now wished the whole family would come rushing down. I was sure I was going to die, my punishment for gluttony. They would find me dead beside my bowl of shredded wheat.

Somehow I managed to crawl up the stairs with thoughts of waking a brother for help. Reaching out with an almost useless arm, I touched the wrong brother— Teedy always talked in pig latin for ten minutes before he was fully conscious. Fortunately his gibberish woke Murray and Billy. Concerned, they asked what was the matter. Pointing in charade fashion to the cause and effect, downstairs to the cause and to my chest as the effect, they rushed down to see what had caused my distress. I followed weakly.

Spying the package of cereal, they each grabbed a bowl, threw in some shredded wheat, and smothered it with milk and sugar, while a contented look spread over their faces. Not caring if I lived or died, they nonchalantly asked where I had gotten it while they licked up every whole wheat thread, throwing the empty package in the old coal range. I couldn't answer them as I was still having difficulty breathing. It was good to know your family would come through for you like that in your time of need.

Eventually I was able to restore my normal breathing. Thereafter if my odd pennies ever amounted to fifteen cents, I always steered clear of that package with Niagara Falls slopping all over it.

Teedy's Tongue

With such a large family, someone was always getting hurt but by far the most accident-prone was Teedy. Once, while playing on the cliffs with our collie, he found some jumping fun for the dog. He would hold an old rag in the air above Prince's head, and Prince would jump savagely to bite at it. Teedy had a bad habit of holding his tongue between his teeth when engaged in any strenuous work or play, and Ma and Pa had warned him against this many times. Teedy at one point held the rag much higher than himself, Prince leaped up—right under his chin—and Teedy's teeth went through his tongue leaving only a rib of it hanging. No one was home as Pa and Ma were out visiting. Ted, holding the biggest part of his tongue in his hand, blood all over him, and with us wanting to pull the remaining thread off, kept asking: "Will I die, will I die?" They were the only words he could say with a mouth full of blood.

Murray ran home and got the lady next door to come down and see what she could do. After seeing the shape Teedy was in, she said "Don't bite the rest off," got him to hold the bitten tongue in the palm of his hand, and headed for home about three blocks away.

Doctor Archibald was called. We were in the background wondering when Pa would find out, who and which one of us would be blamed. We had fast service those days; the doctor only lived about ten blocks away. Rushing into the house, he pulled out the kitchen table and between Teedy's sobs lifted him onto the table, gave him a shot of chloroform, and in

63

seconds Teedy was out like a light. He did a great job of sewing the tongue together and left orders for Teedy not to have anything except fluids through a straw for at least ten days (which gave us a little more bulk food at our table).

When Ma and Pa entered the house the smell of doctor was all over the kitchen, and Pa got so excited he never knew who to blame it on, the dog or us.

Teedy's tongue healed well and he never even had a lisp. It didn't take us long after his tongue was better and he was able to fight and argue with us to christen him with a new name which he despised: "Parrot Tongue".

You Broke My Back
Another time Teedy didn't fare too well was one day when he and I decided to display a few acrobatic tricks we had learned. One of these was the caterpillar, in which I stood straight while he locked his legs around me as high up as he could. Then he would bend his body backwards down the length of my body until he could grasp my ankles with his hands. At this point I was to go down on all fours, allowing his head to continue through my legs. This is very dangerous if done carelessly and as usual that was the way we did it. As soon as he grabbed my ankles in his upsidedown position, I fell, and the weight of my frame came down on Teedy's poor defenseless back. I heard something snap, and it was much louder than his braces. He climbed to his feet without a grunt but looking very frightened, pointed at me and said in a sombre voice, "You broke my back." He didn't have to tell me as I had heard the crack and was more worried than he.

After this remark, he made for an old shed. He ran inside, locked the door, and left me to wait for the results. What could I do? I couldn't go in and tell Pa: "I just broke your son's back, and he has locked himself in the shed to die." With an hour passing, everything silent and still locked, I was wondering if he was still living. I had to get in to him. There was a small opening about nine inches by nine inches. I tried to crawl in through this and got caught. I could see Ted though. He was sitting on an old chair with his top bare, rubbing his spine, not crying, but with a look of death on his face. I was sure I was in worse shape than he was, as I now had half a shoulder in and couldn't move my arm. I was the one who needed help fast, but it was some time before I could get him to even look in my direction. After nearly forty minutes, Ted began to dress. I could see he still had use of his hands and legs, while my arm was going to sleep and needles and pins were taking over. I figured the only way to convince Ted I only had a few hours left was to cry, so I started – really hard at first – but couldn't afford too much loss of energy, as I figured I'd never get out of there. Ted finally stood on his feet and headed sloppily for the door. I breathed, "Get a saw fast and don't be too long, I'm numb." Ted heard my cries, snapped out of his trance, and ran in the house for a saw. I didn't move while he was gone in case I got in a worse tangle. Arriving with a saw that wouldn't have cut hot butter, he commenced to saw the opening larger. Ted had forgotten about his back and kept the saw going furiously through nails and stone shingles. After a few minutes I gave what I thought was the last heave I had left in my body. My arm moved inside. That was a relief, although the other hand was still outside. Finally Teedy sawed a square the size of my body and I was loose. The two of us walked away comparing our sore spots, with me thanking heaven I didn't have to announce to Pa that I had broken his son's back and Teedy thankful he didn't have to tell Pa that he had been the cause of me suffocating in the barn hole.

The Dwarf Is Under the Covers With Me

Each of us had quite a hard time with the old-fashioned flu, which always seemed to hit in early September when the baseball playoffs were the main event. I've never since witnessed the fevers that Teedy, Billy, Murray, and I endured, with each of us seeing the same visions in our fevered brains.

I could easily diagnose my symptoms and, bones aching, freezing and weak, I would zig-zag my way home from the game to an empty house. For a change, food was the last thing

I wanted to see – just water and bed with plenty of blankets, though the temperature was in the seventies.

During one of these flu sieges I stumbled in, took a long drink of water, wobbled upstairs, robbed another bed's clothes, and threw them over the bed I was to die in. In no time I was asleep, drenched in sweat. How I hated to wake up from this first sleep – I knew what was waiting for me.

When I'd wake up from that first drugged sleep in my delirium, it seemed the whole room was filled with water dashing around the bed, with more and more water coming in. I'd have one heck of a time holding on. During this opening scene, I'd sit on the edge of the bed, knowing I was really delirious with fever. I'd think to myself, "Don't be scared; I've seen this before." But I was never too brave, though there was nothing to do but sit and bear with it.

When the water got too high, I'd get under the covers again and sleep for seconds only to awaken to the second act. Now there were all kinds of midgets and dwarfs (looking like the ones on Wrigley's gum years ago) clamouring over the walls and acting like fools. They were very active, and each one had their eyes on me. I'd pull the covers over my head, but there always seemed to be a small gap in the bedclothes where one would peek in at me with a crazy smile.

After a while the dwarfs would leave the room; and then as though I had become a wonderful artist, I'd paint pretty figures in bright colours on the board walls. They seemed beautiful to look at, but you had to look fast before this witch with four protruding teeth, dressed in a black cape, would brush it off the wall with a "tee-hee-hee". I'd sit up and watch this act with the witch until she left the scene. The sequence was always the same with each flu bout – water, dwarfs, picture, witch. The witch part always waited for dusk and I would try to keep in the centre of the bed but it seemed I was forever falling out.

This time the sound of voices broke up the act. My brothers were downstairs, not knowing I was upstairs in an unlighted room and very sick. I heard dishes being transferred to the dishpan. With little strength I reached a shaky arm for one of my boots. Tap, tap, tap on the floor. Downstairs everything was quiet now. I heard: "Who's upstairs?" I was too feeble to answer, and this started a real mystery with them; they wouldn't come upstairs. I was a ghost. So there I lay, parched, waiting for water.

The old dog began to bark. Pa was on his way home from the neighbour's. This made my brothers brave again. They all began to creep upstairs, preparing for an intruder.

I tapped on the floor again to let them know what room I was in. At last they found me in heavy fever– delirious. The doctor was called. He gave me some pills but my hysterical dreams still continued. The night was a month.

Next morning, the faithful doctor came again with a different pill. This one did the trick. My yearly fever flu was almost gone. Within a week or two of my experience another brother would be stricken, and hard as it is to believe, would go through the same scenes in his fevered mind that I had. Teedy though was a bit different. He was a cuddly patient, and when his act started he would jump out of bed, come downstairs, and jump on any lap that was vacant.

I was always too sick to make it downstairs and was obliged to stay in that bedroom with those damn dwarfs jumping all over my bed.

Sulphur and Molasses

In the spring of the year, every kind of sickness was on the go: croup, mumps, scarlet fever, and the killer, spinal meningitis, which we were all waiting to attack us. We thought measles only came to you once, but we had them a dozen times.

Pink eye was a forerunner to the measles. You'd wake up in the morning and through your sticky eyelids, you could barely see it was daylight. Most of us got a bad case of claustrophobia, and we would tear at our eyelids trying to get our breathing started. After we stopped tearing, a few hysterical cries would come from one or two of us. You couldn't see who it was, but we knew each others' voices.

Ma would be waiting for us to come downstairs. Led down by the oldest blind brother, we tagged along, the flap of our long johns open with the ever-so-black ring around the shin of the leg (caused from irritation by the wet sock at the top of the lumberman's rubber). Style meant nothing at this hectic moment. It was "Get my eyes open first, or else you'll have a corpse on your hands." A cup of molasses, a spoon, a box of sulphur, and a bowl of boric acid were on Dr. Ma's table. First, she would grab the sleeve of a little torn shirt, dip it in the boric acid, and rub your eyes. It wouldn't be long before you were able to open one eye. At that moment, with the other eye still not opened, we'd think of the neighbour next door with only one eye and how many times we had imitated him and laughed. But we wouldn't laugh about him this time, at least until we had both eyes opened.

Next treatment was for the blood. We loved the tablespoon of molasses, but that tablespoon of dry sulphur was our worst enemy, and it came last. But it had to go down, or you'd get another one. How happy we were that Ma was the disherouter instead of Pa. We were able to whine with Ma, but Pa would have winged you if you had even made a purr. This went on twice weekly for a few months. The sulphur would work its way through the pores, and after a day's carrying on, we would strip our underwear off and shake the sulphur out.

Ted, the smallest one but with the largest underwear, would be smoking amidst a pile of sulphur in a small heap on the floor. We never caught many colds after that recipe.

Salt Porking Fad

Something else that was all the rage in family medical remedies was the salt porking fad, used when you stuck a nail in your foot. And many a rusty one we stuck in ours— there was no tetanus shot, and it was terribly sore for days. Sometimes you'd diagnose your own case as critical when you spotted a red streak running up your leg and a lump under the bend of your knee. This called for a visit to the doctor, with orders from the whole household to make sure your sore foot was clean.

We knew the exact drawer the doctor would go to for the poison tablets because we were there often with any little ailment, since pills were free to miners and their families. The pills were as large as a peppermint and robin-egg blue; and during one of our hunger spells, we weren't too hesitant about eating one. If it hadn't been for the word POISON grooved across the face of the pill, I think we would have.

This pill was dissolved in hot water every hour, usually in the hand dish or if someone was using that, a dipper. The hotter the better were the doctor's orders. But he didn't know about circumstances at home— that someone had just used all the hot water for tea and you couldn't wait for the kettle to boil on the coal stove, especially when it was a poor draft day.

The tablets having eliminated the red streak on the leg, we'd get the salt pork for the foot. What a job trying to hold it over the nail hole.

A two-inch square of it covered the penetration along with a rag given to you by an angry brother, after a sister had torn a piece off the tail of his only white shirt. This could be smoothed over by telling him the doctor had said you might have to have your leg taken off. Tying the rag so that it wouldn't come off was a contractor's job. The poor sock had a chore to keep the bean pork over the wound. Then on went one bald-headed gum rubber. (If it hadn't been so bald, the nail would never have penetrated the foot.)

Well, off you went, but the pork would come off after about ten steps. Yet you'd continue all day, still fiercely lame. Lifting the foot up from the standing position and shaking it painfully, you could feel that pork from stem to stern, but felt relieved when it hit dead centre.

We were told night time was the best time for the pork to heal and draw the poison, but how could a two-inch square of pig do any healing and drawing when you had to get in bed with seven other lively legs. After the sandman had opened all mouths and closed all eyes, you hardly knew where the ill foot was. In the morning, for the first few seconds on awakening, you never knew you had a sore foot, until you gave a healthy stretch, if there was room. Then touching the good foot with the sore one, you'd find everything was gone, pork, rag, and all. Trying to find it all was taking a chance of having your teeth knocked out by disarranged feet flying around the bed. You'd finally tell your brothers to get up till you found your pork and you'd see a dazed look on their faces, as they were barely awake, wondering what you were talking about. You'd remind them of your sore foot.

It wasn't easy to get another piece of pork, as the last piece had been used up the night before by a sister making a pot of beans, and of course Ted would never consider giving another piece of his shirt tail, and so the hunt would be on. Finally, Murray came up with the pork, all soft and sticky from the heat of Bill's back. The rag was last to be found after searching blankets, bed, etc.—under the bed. You were satisfied now to go on with the cure till the pork got hard and brown and the rag was in shreds. Then you'd know your foot was on the mend.

Six

Boonies, Lamps, Freezing Pipes, and Coal Stoves

The Night Billy Cooked the Pot
In those early years, we had good tap water in our house, but no toilet. Our boonie was about ninety feet from the house, and it had to be kept immaculate. Pa's strict orders were for us to scrub it daily. The Eaton's sale, winter, or Christmas catalogue was nailed on the left of the seat because Pa was left-handed. He didn't care if we did the splits trying to reach it.

In winter the snow would drift thirteen to fifteen feet high all the way to the boonie, but by some act of God the toilet was clear of snow about three feet all around. After we had shimmied open the frozen door and gone inside, the big weighted pulley would slam the door shut. (In summer months, the sudden impact of this hundred pound stone meant instant death to ants, flys, and snakes that cavorted around the outhouse.)

Once inside we would stand on the seat over the hole as it was just too cold to sit down. We had to listen in case Pa was in the vicinity, as standing over the hole was definitely forbidden, and if he had ever caught us, he probably would have pushed us in. But with the fifteen-foot drifts all along the path, we were pretty safe. With Pa's heavy frame, we could hear him bellow as he sank into the drifts.

Braces were a hindrance at such times. Those miserable little braces, which were always buttoned wrong, would sometimes hold up production until it was becoming really serious. The heavy odorous underwear with the escape hatch in the rear (in case of fire from the sulphur and molasses we'd taken all winter long) had to be cleared for an opening for the posterior.

This was done with sighs and groans, wondering if it was all going to be in vain. Were you going to make it in time? At last your rear would make it through the layers of braces and clothing and with all valves in operation, you'd get that faraway look in your eye as the song "When It's Springtime in the Rockies" floated through your brain. The catalogue with the pages running towards the floor hung firmly on a two-inch spike. We never used the ladies' coats page. It was too colourful—a real pleasure to look at, as though we had company right there with us. At the end of our sitting we would turn to the index where a softer paper was used and where we had from A to Z to choose from.

On the way back you'd find yourself skimming over those huge banks like a mole.

For nightly use, we had small enamelled pots under each bed, which were limited to liquid waste only. This had to be disposed of as soon as we woke up next morning.

One night, Billy, who had been eating laxative foods all day, was immediately summoned. It was bitterly cold and he thought he would take a chance and use the hardware under the bed. Ma and Pa were downstairs playing cards. Just as he was finishing he heard Pa's footsteps on the stairs. Taken by surprise, he grabbed pot and contents and stuck them in the oven of the upstairs cookstove. He streaked into bed and waited for the outcry, but it didn't come. Pa just put some more coal on, stoked the stove for the night, and through habit opened the oven door so that the rooms would get the heat stored up inside. What we got wasn't heat. A gagging noise came from Ma, who at once knew what had happened. Soon the fumes filtered into Pa's room. We heard him leap from bed.

He ran through the upstairs, opening every window in the sub-zero weather, trying to entice the foul air to escape. Ma was the type who would speak no more of such an error, but Pa would take it to a judge and jury. This night though because of the fumes he never opened his mouth, and so the sentence had to be postponed until morning. This was a comforting thought to sleep on along with red noses and white ears from the cold.

The Double-Holer
But the old outhouse had seen its day, and its rears. And Pa began building a new one— a double-holer, which around our end of town put us on a level with the elite. We were so excited waiting for it to be constructed that we even held back for two or three days, knowing we'd have company while in progress.

Everything was in pairs to coincide with the double-holer—even two of the latest catalogues, hanging in spots not much farther than the length of your elbow. There were hooked mats on the floor and wallpaper on the walls (which wasn't to be used under any circumstance). Arm rests were nailed on both sides of the openings, which even Henry Ford forgot to put on his first cars. A foot rest on each side was the only mistake, because after you were harnessed into your position, arms under chin and feet on the foot rest, slumbering symptoms took over.

That held up production. We never ever wanted Pa to catch us in this state, especially two brothers at once, as we knew we'd lose all priority. Why Pa never built a waiting room had me baffled. It's an achy feeling when there are four in a building of this size, two on and two waiting with a hurry up-hurry up attitude on their faces. Sometimes Ted would give you a warning without speaking. Then you knew you had to jump off in a hurry or be sorry for it. Ted's face would get blood red and his breathing would subside; then at the last minute, he'd shiver and we knew we had to get out of the way fast.

This building wasn't partitioned for the sexes, nor did it

have a sign to represent the distinction. We were forbidden to attend a session while Ma or our sisters were in conference. Had we known of any union at that time to fight for our rights, we would have gladly consulted it, especially in early autumn with the green apples half-ripened.

Whenever we'd see a brother running like a scalded cat towards the outhouse, we'd automatically accompany him, sit next to him, and swap yarns as though we were on the CPR first class. It had that train effect on us.

Many a head would peek through the curtain if by chance the preacher or a salesman was on his way to the outhouse. We'd peek patiently, hoping he wouldn't mistake the henhouse for the boonie, and try our best to eliminate the thought that one of us should go with him to accompany him on the spare hole.

At times our homework was taken out there. There we'd sit, in dead earnest, long wrinkled pant legs resting on the foot rest. It was a good environment to be in to get away from Pa and study your lessons in peace.

To friends of ours who had one-holers, we four brothers would brag and say very proudly, "We have a two-holer." It was the same as if their father had a Ford and Pa had a Cadillac.

Don't Spit On the Lamp

As for most people without flush toilets, we also had no electricity for quite a few years. You may wonder how we could get into trouble with Pa in the lamp area, but as we had only one lamp in the kitchen for us to study by while Pa read his paper, this wasn't too hard. While we were spread around the table doing our lessons, with Pa sitting in the old rocking chair, what a job it was to keep our head shadows off his paper. We couldn't make a mistake and blur his reading even for a second.

While attempting to go to the sink for a drink, we would try every strategy to get clear of Pa's paper. We would duck and throw our head in the opposite direction. If we were lucky in the placing of our shadow, nothing was said; but most times we were sent to bed for that careless but unavoidable mistake. If only we could have been given lessons in how not to cast a shadow.

Each night waiting for Pa to finish his paper was like being in a trap, because after he read it, he would get his pencil and proceed to do the crossword puzzle. But we soon got wise as to the best place to sit during this stage. Stationing ourselves close to the sink, we could avoid sending bogeyman shadows over his paper. It was hard to read a book twelve feet from a lamp, but we did it.

One night as we circled the lamp like moths, with Pa in his usual not-too-humorous mood, Billy, tired of studying, was experimenting with the lamp quietly so as not to draw Pa's attention from his reading. He spit a small splash on the lampshade and—crack—the shade broke and a piece fell out, which caused the flame to run wild on the sides of the lamp. Visibility was only two feet now with Pa four feet from the table.

A roar came from Pa. He flew at us, and we all received a couple of hard belts on our rears with another early night in bed. (This going to bed early most nights made things quite embarrassing for us as friends used to phone and ask to speak to one of us, only to be told we were in bed a few hours after school. They thought we were some kind of freaks. But we would fix it up next day by telling our friend we had overeaten and had felt drowsy. Instead, we'd had no supper and it would be about 4 a.m. before we'd even close an eye.)

I also had a mishap with the lamp. One quiet day when everyone was out of the house, I decided to look up in the attic to see what things Pa had saved from his youth. The attic was supposed to be out of bounds to us— the only time we were legally allowed to be there was Christmas to pick up the same year-after-year decorations.

There was no floor. A six-inch-wide board ran across the opening of the attic. To straddle those two-by-four rafters in the dark was a talent in itself if you walked them correctly without a plunge. I held onto the body of the lamp and attempted my trapeze act. Trying to prevent a fire in the attic, my attention was focused on the lamp and the tinder-dry collections accumulated there, not thinking how many bones I'd break if I fell.

Naturally, it wasn't long before I missed my footing and dropped through to the room below, with the lamp minus its shade burning furiously. After doing a complete flip-flop, I landed in an upright position, my body wracked with pain. Somehow I had managed to keep the lamp intact, though a few small fires were breaking out around me. I couldn't do anything about them until I got back my faculties. Finally I came to my senses, blew out the lamp, and extinguished the small flare-ups. I had no time for anything except to go downstairs and plan how to get a lamp shade, with no extras in the house and the price for a new one eighteen cents.

Bill had a paper route and I had heard him say a Mr. Brown owed him eighteen cents for the daily paper. This stood out clearly in my mind as I waddled my sore limbs to his house about a mile away. With barely enough skin left on my knuckles to knock, I rapped with the tips of my fingers.

In a few minutes the door was opened and an innocent voice was saying, "My brother sent me over for the eighteen cents, so he can turn the money in tonight." Falling for the sad look I displayed, he reached in his pocket and gave me the money he owed Bill. I scooted for home as I had to buy a lamp shade and get the mess cleaned up before Pa arrived from the mine.

I did a great job of cleaning up, at the same time thinking that that was the last tightrope walking I would do until a floor was laid.

The only thing I had to contend with now was Bill's reaction to my invading his paper route money. But after reminding him of a few crooked deals he had dealt me, he became quite agreeable.

Oh, To Be a Camel, So We Could Fill Our Humps

When the temperature dipped below the zero mark in the winter, Pa would turn off the water in the tap with a small crank. He would tell us beforehand that he was going to turn off the water for the night and figured we'd quench our thirst. At the time he told us we weren't the least bit thirsty, but just as soon as he'd get that little rusty crank in his hand to give the nut a turn, our throats would be parched. Of course we didn't dare tell Pa this as he'd given us plenty of notice and would have turned us off for the night if we'd told him we wanted some water then.

Hours later, we'd trudge up to bed with a foamy saliva frothing in our mouths, wondering if we'd live till morning when the water would be turned on again.

One night we were so thirsty, we waited until Pa had gone to bed and gave him an hour to fall asleep; then Billy and I made for the downstairs very quietly, as dry as poisoned rats. We got our much-needed water, but then made the mistake of not turning the shut-off completely off this bitterly cold night.

Next morning, as usual, Pa gave the crank a turn and waited for the water to come trickling out. Instead, nothing came—not a drop. Billy and I looked at each other sheepishly behind Pa's back. This meant the pipes were frozen. I knew what came next.

Under Pa's orders, down I crawled into the three-foot-deep cellar with an armful of newspapers and matches and scrunched along for about thirty feet until I found the pipes. There were three pipes running to the well, and it was quite a trick to figure out which one needed the heat. This was the only time when we were commandeered by Pa that we didn't care what he said because we were far out of his reach. I'd roll the newspaper up tightly, light one end, and run the flame up and down the length of galvanized pipe. (It's a wonder I never set the house on fire as the floor above the old pipes was cobwebbed and tinder dry.) I'd hear Pa's voice from the kitchen,

"Hope you're applying the heat to the centre pipe." "Yes sir," I'd holler up, as I jumped from the end pipe to the centre pipe.

Freezing, choking, and eyes smarting, I'd keep up this process for half an hour. Then I'd hear from Pa, "It must have been a cold night. I've never known it to freeze like that before, once it was shut off. Come on up, it's starting to drip."

We boys never did learn to turn the water off right, and so in future we never attempted another drink after Pa closed it off for the night. We just made sure that when Pa asked, "Anyone want water?" that we had a drink then whether we needed it or not.

Seven

Our Adventures With the Animal Kingdom

The Sad Death
We were always told that small birds like sparrows and grey birds might be our youngest brother who had died when he was just a baby. We were disappointed many times when, calling a bird by our brother's name, it would fly away. I tried every sneaky way to get up to one of those sweet things to have a good talk with it about my baby brother. If it were alone and flew away, we'd make excuses to each other, saying: "It's gone to get some more little birds, so it won't be scared." We weren't fast enough to catch a lively one, but were always on the look out for a crippled or dead one. When we came across one, no matter how far from home, we'd gently carry it to the house.

One afternoon as I was walking along the shores I stumbled upon a little grey bird with its wing badly cut. I was glad it was hurt as I could catch it without trouble. Caressing it gently, I crawled up the steep cliff to return home, talking to it from the minute I found it. I told it I would cure it.

Small samples of Mecca ointment used to be delivered free house-to-house, one to a family; and as we had a large house, we'd manage to get three for the other two tenants who weren't there. Those small cans of ointment were for cuts and bruises. This is what I would put on the bird's wound.

No one was home and I was the head surgeon, using the whole can on the one wing, absolutely sure this would fix him up. After the operation, I found a lovely place outdoors, rounded a small nest in the deep grass, and left it for a while.

I was deliriously happy and kept thinking that when the bird was better, I'd give it a good talking to about my brother. I wasn't going to tell a soul about the little bird at first, but I was too happy to keep it a secret. One of my sisters coaxed me to show her my prize. To surprise her even more I said, "You go around the back and wait; I'll go and get it." Out to the deep grass I tramped. Not knowing the exact spot, I felt a squashing and slipping under my stompers, and I looked down to find I had flattened the little bird. If somebody had hollered in my ear, I wouldn't have heard. Down I plunked in the grass with the pitiful-looking little bird in my hand. What could I tell my sister? Drawn by my loud sobs, she came around the corner of the house. Seeing what had happened, she reasoned with me that it was probably dead even before I had trampled it. But that didn't pacify me. I took him in the house, got some butter on a spoon, heated it over the coal stove, and tried to spoon some into his ruptured beak, still praying he might live.

After keeping him good and warm for hours, waiting for a miracle, my brothers came home and persuaded me that it was no use, and they helped me give that dear little bird, that might have been our baby brother, a lovely burial.

You Smell Like Wet Feathers

Most kids are hung up on something. When I was about twelve my hang-up was pigeons. I studied them constantly— I knew each pigeon's origin, whether it lived in the eaves of the church or the school or was privately owned. I recognized them when perching around on the town square and could detect their colours when in flight. I'm sure many times they were watching me because they usually took an extra dip when they flew over my head.

One miserable sleeting day as I was on my way to school, I

spotted a pigeon huddled at one corner of the school house. My heart skipped a beat. It was as if I had found gold, only I would rather have had the pigeon than the gold. I walked towards it amazed that it didn't fly away. Then I noticed it was covered with ice. It must have weighed ten pounds, twelve ounces of pigeon and the rest ice.

How was I going to keep that pigeon until noon when I could take it home? I knew if I left it there, someone would take it; and if I came back at noon to find it gone, I'd regret it the rest of my life.

I quickly made up my mind— to hell with school (very unlike me). I'll grab that chubby bird and take it home. I placed the ice-covered pigeon inside my shirt and my Stanfield long johns. Cold and wet from the pigeon's melting coat of ice, I approached our house from the back entrance in order to get to the henhouse without being seen. Luck was with me as the windows on that side of the house were frosted up. This meant Pa couldn't see the commotion.

The pigeon's icy overcoat was completely melted when I plucked him from my underwear. Everything was going fine— even the hens, which Pa had bought recently, seemed to be in on the act, looking secretively at the pigeon. Then their little brown eyes would stare at me as if to say, "That's an odd bird you got there." I began to have a guilty conscience in front of the hens, as though they knew I was supposed to be in school. But they made little noise, somehow sensing that if Pa found out I was there, they'd suffer also.

But what a mess I was left with in my underwear. I hadn't realized the pigeon's vital organs would start working when the ice melted, but work they had. I cleaned myself as best I could, then hid in the henhouse until noon, stroking and fondling my fat little friend. At lunchtime, I slipped in the house and sat at the table with the rest, feeling very happy, knowing I was the owner of a real live pigeon.

I had a few complaints from Billy that I smelled like wet feathers, but passed it off saying it was the material in the jacket I was wearing.

I had that pigeon for nearly a week, feeding him the best food available to restore his strength. Then one day, assured he would return to me, I gave him his freedom. You never saw a bird take off so fast. He made a bee line for the school, without the least bit of thanks to me. In fact I think I heard him say "Dummy", as he whirred out of my hand like a shot from a slingshot.

I never could understand why a pigeon would prefer the schoolhouse to the henhouse, when I hated it so much.

Each time I went to school after that, I could spot him among the rest; but all he would give me was a sideways glance, and after all the mess he'd made in my underwear too.

The Unclucked Hen

Not only was I crazy about pigeons, but Teedy and I were both nuts about setting hens too. One day our obsession for a setting hen was finally attained.

Teedy and I bought a black hen with white spots for a dollar. We were certain we had bought ourselves a setting hen. At twelve I guess I thought all hens were setting hens. But it didn't cluck like one. That didn't worry me though. I thought, "I'll make you cluck, you little dear."

We fixed up an old shack for it to set in and scraped up 35 cents to buy thirteen setting eggs for the unclucked hen. Cautiously I settled the hen over her precious unborn family. She looked at me as if to say, "What are you doing with me?" She didn't appear very willing to sit on them, so again I gently seated her over the eggs. I pressed on her shoulders until her legs gave out and continued pressing– not too hard– but just until the weight was too much for her. Finally she must have decided the pressure was too great and she sat down on them. I kept my hands on her for a while to make sure she wouldn't get up again. Not daring to breathe I took my hands off and stayed there a while. She remained on the eggs, and then took a piece of hay in her beak and threw it over her shoulder. To Teedy and I, this was a sure sign. We would have chicks. Whispering, we decided we should go outside and leave her alone. We walked around like expectant fathers thinking of our pregnant hen. We couldn't get over this miracle. With thoughts of chickens to come, we were walking on air, hardly able to speak to each other. To think we had paid only one dollar for the hen. Why, we would soon be multi-millionaires.

Then our curiosity overwhelmed us again and we peeked through a tiny hole on the left of the barn to see how the hen was doing. She was still there, throwing hay over her back. This was history in the making, and it puffed us up again with the thrill of it all. This time we had a consultation and decided not to go near her for at least an hour.

Just as we were deciding where to put the chicken coop I said to Teedy, "I just have to take one more look. Then we'll go and have something to eat." I looked through the little hole once more and saw that the whole face of the black hen was yellow. I beckoned to Teedy to look too. Then we both rushed inside to check on this peculiar occurrence. There she sat, the cannibal, with egg all over her face and not the least bit ashamed. This mother, who had performed infanticide when we weren't looking, had eaten all the eggs but four and was getting ready to dive into the remaining ones.

I had never beaten a hen before, and I didn't know where to start. But I beat it and beat it, hitting it everywhere I could think. The best spot seemed to be on its back, but my hand kept bouncing back up to me. The hen's eyes questioned, "What in hell are you doing now," while I was imagining how she'd taste in a stew.

Playing Cow

Something else that really turned us on were cows. We hardly ever saw one around Sydney Mines, but when we did, we would study it from all angles watching every move it made.

Its every mannerism was recorded in our brain. I guess it was from our preoccupation with cow life that our cow pageant was derived.

We developed this form of play in our early years. As soon as Pa and Ma would go out, we felt as though we were experiencing a holiday from school on a warm day. They wouldn't be fifty feet from the house, when we'd begin to arrange the scene. A small cubby hole below the pantry was our stall. Four of us boys got in there snuggly tight. A large bread board about 3 feet by 3 feet closed off the hole, and when we were ready to go out to pasture, one of us cows would have to act like a farmer, just for a few minutes, and open the gate to let us out. Two basins of water were placed on the floor in front of the cubby hole, and when the farmer would let us out (afterwards turning right back into a cow), we'd amble leisurely along the kitchen floor on all fours. Going in separate directions, we eventually all ended up at the water trough and would wait in line until the cow in front was satisfied, patiently licking each other's face or neck while he was drinking.

Each of us had one of Ma's long cashmere stockings pinned to our behind, and we would swish our tails amiably. There was never any laughter at these times. We were deadly serious cows in the highest sense of the word. Mooing played a definite part in our performance. Other than that, everything was strolling about and licking; the only time the silence was broken was when we couldn't get out a good moo. It's pretty hard to do a good clean moo that really sounds like a cow's.

The longer we played, the more we advanced into the cow state. We could even scratch like a cow with the hind leg. Billy, the oldest, usually acted not only as a cow, but also as the farmer and shepherd: and if it was a fine night, he would open the back door and out we would stroll, down the stone steps and over to the grass. There we would eat, moo, lick, scratch, then lay down and do a bit of cud chewing.

Swallowing that green grass wasn't too tasty, but with our brains working in cow language, we'd chew it up as if it were candy. Our knees would get tired, but it would continue for hours. Finally, when filled with water and grass and rest, Billy would lead us in cow fashion up the stone steps, back through the kitchen, and into our little cubby hole. Then we'd begin speaking one by one and come out of our cow trance. In the morning, we were almost ready to be milked.

Catch Her On the Squat

As we got older, someone pastured a few cows in a field beside us. Our garden wasn't much bigger than the kitchen, but Pa wanted it well fertilized. To the pasture we went, with four buckets and a shovel to gather up the manure for the garden. As soon as one bucket was sloshed full with fresh cow manure, it would be carried a good distance by one of us boys to enrich Pa's garden.

Many a time a poor unmilked cow, in the process of a good bowel movement, wondering if we were going to milk it at this stage of the game, would see one of us trying to catch its droppings in the bucket before hitting the ground. It was easier this way than trying to scoop it into the bucket with the shovel, especially when it landed in six inches of grass. Three or four day old stuff was easily plopped into the bucket by hand, as it had formed a crust and it was as though you were lifting a fluffy pancake to place on your plate.

Quite cool in the early spring, there was always a watchful brother, a shepherd in a sense, keeping an eye on all movements of the cows. A signal was shouted at any instant, whenever a cow had just peed or was spotted in the squatting position. Buckets were laid down on the ground and all four of us would run in the direction of the cow, shooing her away, taking over her spot, and standing in the hot bladder waste to relieve the numbness in our feet. A beautiful feeling of warmth, while it was still warm. There was only one after-effect we never liked— the itching of the feet when they began drying off; but this was soon remedied by scuffing our feet through the long damp grass, then grabbing our buckets and finding new piles.

After the cow field was emptied, we loved the adventure of cleaning up the horse pasture; and the scent of the horse manure was heaven to our noses. We commenced to fill our buckets. No shovel was needed for these pellets. When a new pile was found a fierce battle would rage, and as Teedy always had the habit of keeping his mouth open, Bill once made a hole-in-one. After cleaning Teedy's mouth out the best we could, the regiment was at ease. It was almost a shame to put those beautiful grenades in the bucket, but Pa was waiting behind the tall trees, not dreaming his four elves were whooping it up.

There was a foot of manure covering our small garden from end to end. When planting time came, the poor seeds looked as though you were treating them wrong, planting them in manure with the earth a foot below. It must have been all the coal dust in the mud that limited growth, because even with the thick spreading of manure, Pa never had much of a garden.

But Pa still seemed proud when out of a whole package of radish seed, only three or four came shyly up, even though their leaves looked around as if to say, "Well, will you look at how many of us actually made it up?"

The Purified Pig
We had a cure-all for cuts, boils, etc., called P & G soap (at four cents a pound). We would make a poultice of it by gumming it to a paste with a table knife and adding a tablespoon of sugar. After applying it, it would not only draw a boil, but the Brooklyn Bridge out of the water as well. It was a great feeling mashing up the P & G soap, which had been heated first to soften it. Mixing the sugar and soap in the palm of your hand with its fudge-like appearance, you'd catch yourself almost eating it.

One evening when I had applied the poultice to a wound, my thoughts wandered to our neighbour's pig. I still had a lot of the mixture left, and it was a shame to waste something that looked as tasty as that. I darted across to where the pig was kept and stuck it in his face, thinking he would probably turn his snout up at it, but to my surprise he grabbed it and downed it, grunting good-naturedly as if he thought it was ice cream. I ran home and told no one what I had done, thinking the pig might die any minute. The next few days I kept an eagle eye on the pen to see if the pig still had its equilibrium. It seemed to be more alert and friendly than I'd ever seen a pig.

About three days after the pig's cleanest meal, the neighbour lady said to me out of a clear blue sky, "You know Sewey is a different pig. She was sick for a couple of weeks – wouldn't eat and just moped around, but the last couple of days she's been eating good and seems real perky." Not saying anything about my doctoring, I figured I should win the Nobel Pig Prize.

Now if I should ever find anyone who has a sick pig, I won't be as sneaky as I was in those days. I'll just give them a written prescription for P & G soap mixed with sugar – pigs thrive on it.

I Was Attacked By a Dead Pig

In my next experience with a pig, I didn't fare so well. Pa had a pig called John that he had raised from a piglet. I was almost hysterical when the time came to slaughter it. I never wanted to see anything killed, let alone be an accessory to it.

There were two pretty girls visiting our place the day the pig was to meet its doom, and I tried my best to be a "know everything man" to win the love and admiration of these beauties.

Tarzan never swelled with pride more than I did when Pa asked me in front of the girls if I would help him slaughter the pig. If the girls hadn't been there, I would have run away to the shores, escaping the killing and my part in it. Doing everything in my power to show my bravery in front of the girls, I said, "Sure I'll help you."

Chest out, chin tucked in, I followed Pa to the shed. Over his right shoulder he carried a twenty-two rifle. Since I had never witnessed the likes before, Pa gave me the ground rules inside the shed. First off, he took a handful of grain and threw it in John's trough. (A pig is much like my brother Murray: if something is placed on the table, or in the trough, he'd eat it whether it was meal time or not.) What Pa wanted me for was to hold the legs after the pig had been shot so that he could stick it.

I expected to come out of this mission a renowned hero in front of my sweet audience.

Pa rested the end of the rifle between the pig's eyes, and while the pig was licking up the last handful of feed, he pulled the trigger —crack —and the girls gave a piercing screech, holding their hands over their ears.

The pig fell over on one side with one short grunt. It was dead and harmless —or so I thought —and walking out of the shed, I received praise for the bravery I had shown by just being in there. Pa called me back, with orders to roll the pig on its back and hold its legs. Glittering in Pa's hand was a six-inch blade so sharp that you could nick a hair. "Hold her down!" hollered Pa. I straddled the pig, sitting on its hind legs and getting a grip on its front feet, as the girls looked on in awe while false bravery exuded from all my pores.

I had no idea in the world that once it was shot it would ever move again. Pa drove the knife into the pig's throat. Then the struggle started —Pa's idea of me holding the front feet sure was a mistake. I guess he didn't know either as it was the first time he had ever killed a pig. The hind feet started digging, flailing, tearing at my posterior like a propeller on a motor boat. Pa was hollering for me to sit on the hinds, but you can't stop a motor by sitting on it.

Wondering how long this could last, I just knew there was a lot of trouble down behind. Its razor-sharp hooves tore the seat clear off my pants and the skin clear off my rear. Jumping clear of the pig with it still kicking, I backed gingerly towards the shed, never letting my rear parts look on the face of the girls. I had many thoughts running through my mind — one, that I was ruined for life. In the house we had a long mirror. This was what I was racing for in my ragged condition. It wasn't hard to pull my pants off as there wasn't much left in the rear section. Backing up to the mirror and looking over the situation, my breathing slowed.

My clawings and cuts were too many and too fresh to be painful, but I had to tell myself that to believe it wasn't too serious. Had the girls or Pa come in during my "backward performance", I would have turned into a recluse.

Patching those pants was a first class tailor's job, but I tackled the raggedy job anyway. I cut the rear out of a pair of Pa's old pants and sewed on this mammoth patch that hid all scars.

When I was able to get my cords and veins operating from my navel down, I went out into the shed where the astonished girls were watching Pa scalding the pig. Arriving there without too much of a Tarzan attitude, no words were swapped. I watched the expressions on the girls' faces to detect any sign of faltering about my bravery.

When Pa came with the boiling buckets of water, ready to scald the pig, I slinked out of the way, taking no chances – it might still have some life in it and make another last minute attempt to live at my expense.

Pa and the girls took sly looks at my patched rear, when it was exposed to their view accidentally, but my full attention was centred on the boiling hot water splashing over the throatless, gutless pig.

The pig was hanging now by its tendons, with its evil snout pointing to the ground. I brushed my hands together, at the same time peeking at the girls, trying to make them forget that serious half hour when Pa had stuck the pig; and leading them to believe that although I had suffered terrific pain, it was only natural and happened to anyone who killed a pig.

I was hoping that the girls would leave the shed and go on their way, when one of them said, "Mother wants us home at two thirty." With shoulders straight, chin in, and rear end very touchy, I walked stiffly back to the house, with the big mirror in mind in order to have a really good look. I could see the long two-pronged scratches. It would have been easier to tell people I had sat on a rabid octopus lying on its back.

Later, Pa arrived with the pig's liver and heart, put them on a platter, and placed them in the icebox. Asking me about my condition, I was embarrassed to tell him, leaving him to judge for himself. I was dressed with half a flannelette blanket pinned to the inside of the rear patch, which softened the rough feeling of the bulky threads.

Eating off the mantle piece for weeks after that, I dared not sit down. Healing was in progress, itching, sore, and stinging. I frequently had my hand down there nonchalantly feeling the scabs.

In a future conversation with Pa, he asked my opinion whether or not we should get another pig. I told him in a quick lying manner that I had heard that pork had taken a drastic drop in price and that it would be much cheaper to buy one shot, knifed, and already cut up. Pa fell for my answer and told me to take the fence down around the pig shed, which was done immediately before he changed his mind.

Eight

With Ma's Death Come Stricter Rules, Ghosts, and Other Means Of Acquiring Food

Things Change Swiftly

After Pearl was born, Ma started having a lot of trouble with her heart. She had a leaking valve and suffered for years. We could say digitalis when most kids our age thought we were talking in a foreign tongue. Many a night one of us would run downstairs for a pill for Ma. We all seemed to suffer right along with her. As far as letting thoughts that Ma might die enter our minds, we just knew she couldn't. She had many trips to the hospital; and, thinking each to be her last, she would get the four of us younger brothers to promise to take good care of Pearl.

When I was fifteen, Ma was taken seriously ill and rushed to the hospital as before. But this time she went into a coma and never came out. Why God hadn't taken Pa were our silent wonderings. Pa was heart-broken and tried to hide his loss from us; but there would always be a brother who would make a mistake and walk into a room where Pa was sobbing.

Things changed swiftly. Billy, Teedy, Murray, and I were to look after Pearl, who was now seven, as Ma had requested. We had to babysit for her every night; and if we went out, she had to tag right along with us. When hanging around with rough fellows who were cursing and swearing, we'd end up in a fight to keep them quiet so that Pearl wouldn't hear their foul language. We became very protective of her.

The Bunny Rabbit Woman

During our housekeeping years after our mother died, a friend who had been a frequent visitor for years still made her unwelcome sojourn in our house; unwelcome as far as Pa was concerned, because she was a terrible cook. We loved to see her come not only to help with the housekeeping, but also because she told many a tall tale.

She was about five-foot-three and stout all over, with sort of a rabbit face that twitched every now and then from the long straight hair hanging over her face. A top and bottom set of teeth she found hard to keep from dropping out. It seemed to us she always had three sets of teeth in at one time. And she had quick steps like a bunny, thus acquiring the name "Bunny Rabbit" from us.

She had a loving heart and asked us many times to ask Pa to marry her, so that she could be our stepmother. But we kept putting off asking Pa. Pa would much rather eat what we prepared than what she put her hand to. Her husband had died many years before, and people said it was the best move he had ever made.

She lived about twenty-five miles from our house. When we saw her waddling up the road with her little packed satchel, this meant her plans were to stay for a week or two, which we brothers loved. But Pearl was afraid of her and would start crying as soon as she saw her coming.

One evening we saw her waddling through the huge snow drifts like a winter mole. To stop Pearl's crying we told her we would arrange sleeping quarters for the little rabbit woman so that she wouldn't be near her. Being very superstitious at her age, she fit in well with us. But we made the mistake of letting her tell us so many spooky tales this one night that she had to sleep in our room as we were scared stiff.

Rigging a fast cot up for our visitor, pulling it into our room in a corner, and sharing our bedding, plus throwing a few overcoats on her, the night began. What a night! Inside five

92

minutes the snoring started. It was a different snore from the ordinary kind –there was no break-off, just a continuous report. Pa would holler in and say: "Who is singing?", which started us laughing for the night. Giggling and whispering we thought she was just putting it on. Although it was about twenty-eight degrees in our room, Murray went over and put the window next to her up about a foot. It wasn't too long after that that we heard an overcoat drop on the floor – then the sawing subsided, and she gave a call to Bill to put the window down. So he jumped up, closed the window, threw the coat on her, and within seconds the snoring started again. There was nothing to do but sleep with it.

Next morning we reminded her of her loud snoring, and she told us that she only snored in strange beds.

Easter was drawing nigh. Our older brother brought home a twenty-pound turkey for Easter Sunday, so Bunny decided to cook it for us. Pa warned us before he left the house not to let her even touch the turkey. He had more faith in our cooking. As soon as he left she took over. She said, "You boys, don't you dare touch the bird as I've cooked many a turkey in my day." We noticed the first thing she did was wrong. She put the bird in the pan by itself, no grease, water, or anything, and shoved it into the boiling oven, almost driving us across the kitchen. We gave up.

With the fierce fire we had in the stove, the turkey was burnt to a crisp an hour before Pa arrived, and we couldn't salvage enough meat for one person. Knowing her mistake, she said, "Well boys, I'm sorry it happened, but it's nearly time for me to head for home." So after packing her little satchel she left.

After she went we tried every angle to figure a way to tell Pa that we weren't to blame for this mess. After convincing Pa that she had as much as thrown us away from the oven, he waited for the second water to be changed on the salt herring. Bunny stayed away for a month or two, but when she dropped by again, she was elected to do the dishes and scrubbing only.

In the meantime, we were responsible for running the house.

The Brothers, Grim, Become Housekeepers
As Pa went to work at 5 a.m., someone had to get up at four, make the fire, pack his lunch, and get breakfast ready to start his day. He worked from Monday to Friday, except once a month when he had to work on Saturday.

The schedule was drawn up as follows:

> Sunday —Teedy
> Monday —Murray
> Tuesday —Andy
> Wednesday —Bill, head of the household
> Thursday —Murray
> Friday —Andy
> Saturday —Teedy once a month.

The long siege began, winter and summer, with the turns all done without argument, including dish washing and baby sitting for Pearl. Murray, Teedy, Pearl, and I went to school. Billy stayed home and was chief cook and bottle washer. Murray and I made bread on Tuesdays and Fridays, twenty-five to thirty loaves at a time. But Billy did the dainty cooking. Once, he made a sponge cake from a recipe out of a book that was over a hundred years old. He opened the oven and gave a shout for me to look. There, rising out of the centre of the cake was a bubble resembling a mammoth toad. Thoughtlessly, he punched a hole in the middle of it. The scalding steam zipped up his arm. Billy always blamed the failure of his sponge cake on the antiquity of the recipe. But we always felt the volcano was caused by not stirring the baking powder.

Billy was strict in his housekeeping. He'd scrub the house from one end to the other; and, winter or summer, he'd make us take off our shoes before entering. Anything out of place had to be corrected.

He was the only one of the boys who could get along fairly well with Pa, and as a result, took some awful chances that

94

we'd never dare.

In winter, Pa would pack his summer underwear away and in summer, pack away his winter underwear. Billy would wear Pa's winter underwear in the summer and summer underwear in the winter. One morning Pa and I got into an argument while I was getting him ready for work. As the argument grew louder and louder, I heard brother Bill tearing down the stairs to part the pugilists. Then I heard the sound of him tearing right back upstairs again without coming into the kitchen. Eventually we calmed down and Pa went off to work. I scrambled upstairs to see what had happened to my aide-de-camp. He said, "I was just ready to open the door to the kitchen when I realized I was wearing Pa's underwear out of season."

That Great Grabbing Feeling
The worst part about these years was getting up to put Pa off to work.

Precisely at 4:30 a.m., after filling Pa's lunch can, starting the coal fire, and making his breakfast, we were to wake Pa. In that half hour many things ran through our mind. There was the front room, dark and gloomy, and the dining-room to the left of the kitchen, which was "not too rid of ghosts". Our eyes looked neither left nor right. The stove and table were all we cared to see for that half hour.

Meals and lunches were slapped together under great strain. We listened for anything that breathed or coughed, ready to make a dash upstairs for help from the sleeping beauties. When everything was finished, the break had to be made down the long hall and past the darkened front room. To get by there without something grabbing you and hauling you into its lair was a feat in itself. But we were trained to a certain speed. First, the kitchen door was quietly opened so as not to disturb the spooks, then a breakneck charge down the hall, before taking a horseshoe right at the bottom of the fifteen steps. The worst was over then, as the fifteen steps were climbed in three strides and sometimes in two. Each day when I hit the top step, I knew that whatever was going to grab me in that front room was gnashing its teeth in disappointment.

Upstairs, bravery settled over my whole body. Pa was a light sleeper, and so I'd give him a very faint call: "Pa, it's time to get up." Then, knowing Pa was right behind me, I'd stride down those stairs one at a time. Defiantly, I'd look into the front room, into the kitchen, and into the dining-room, as if it were broad daylight. Then Pa would wash up for work, while I put the finishing touches to his hearty breakfast of rolled oats, bacon, and tea. But as soon as Pa was about ten feet from the house on his way to work, the great grabbing feeling would sweep over me. I'd yank the light chain on the run, scurry upstairs, and fly in between three open-mouthed sleepers to warm my icy feet.

One night we had salt herring for dinner. That was the meal —no dessert, nothing else to eat in the house; so we figured we might as well go to bed and dream about a nice dessert. It was only early −8 p.m. −and it was Teedy's turn to get up next morning with Pa. He had the alarm clock beside him. Eventually, we drifted off to sleep. Perhaps it was because of his empty stomach that Teedy woke up at twenty-five past twelve. At any rate, he looked at the clock, thought it said five o'clock, rushed into Pa's room, jolted him awake, and sped downstairs with Pa following close behind. Everything was done in quadruple time by both—no scary feeling for Teedy this morning, as Pa was hopping into his clothes right behind him.

Teedy threw a few sandwiches together and made porridge. Pa, dressing at the same time, ate it standing up. Out into the freezing dark night ran Pa, and of course no sooner was he out the door, than Teedy leaped at the light chain, rushed past the scary room, upstairs, and into bed with us. He received a few insults about his big rear, until his pudgy little body was centred in the best spot on the bed. Ten or fifteen minutes elapsed. Ted was just about to doze off again with his partners when the downstairs door opened and in popped Pa, embarrassed and mad at the early hour he had rehearsed his daily grind. It was now a quarter to 1 a.m. Pa undressed, went back to bed, and never did say too much to Teedy. I guess he figured he was nearly as bad as Teedy was.

Some summer nights we would go to a dance at a yacht club, three miles away. With no means of transportation but the thumb, we'd think it over quite seriously before going, especially if it was our turn to put Pa off to the mine at 4 a.m. Four o'clock comes quite sneakily when the dance is in full swing at one o'clock, with everyone kicking up their heels and enjoying themselves. Then one of your brothers would come to you and say, "Pa doesn't want bread in his lunch can tomorrow; he wants a bran cake." (The one who made up Pa's lunch was responsible for his stomach.) Murray was great at knocking your spirits even lower by saying, "Do you know that if you fell asleep right where you're standing now, you'd only get two and one half hours sleep?" As it was, you'd have three miles to walk home. Then you'd have to make a bran cake, which meant you had to get the coal stove going, which probably saw its last ember at eight o'clock.

A typical scene: You are very tired right now and you are still three miles from home, with no cars in sight. Well that's life and it's my turn to put Pa away for the day. We four all land home together, almost asleep. The brothers are yawning, feeling sorry for my troubles and ribbing me, saying I should come to bed with them, which would be unheard of. Instead here I am, grabbing the Quaker bran box and getting my ingredients ready for a fast bran cake, so that Pa won't have heartburn. Everyone in bed, it's now three-thirty. I don't bother setting the clock for 4 a.m. as it would ring in a half an hour anyway, and there is nothing more agitating than a clock ringing in a quiet kitchen and the one responsible for it with only a few faculties left. So I make one big morning of it and start the porridge for Pa, while the fire is roaring. The rest of the morning is taken up filling the lunch can and getting Pa's rubbers warm.

Just the thought of everyone asleep upstairs and little old

you down here doing your duty, scared to death of every sound, made us very nervous of our old house at that time of the morning. It was wonderful if you could get a breathing creature with you downstairs at this time of morning, even though it might be a cat; but Pa despised cats.

Sometimes we'd come up with an arrangement the night before. I'd say, "If you get up with me tomorrow morning, I'll get up with you at your turn." That was good, if you could make the agreement stick. But when the time came to wake up, it would take a good hour coaxing, but to no avail. In the morning, it would be the same old story, "I never heard ya." Lots of times, if I'd have had the strength, I would have carried a brother down in my arms and just laid him on the sofa. He wouldn't have had to wake up, just be there so that I could have the feeling that someone was with me.

Many a tit I broke on the thermos bottle by being so nervous and jittery on those terrifying mornings. I'd take printer's wax, heat it, and put it on the break, but it didn't do much good as Pa would say his tea was cold, not knowing he had a mended thermos bottle.

In summer it wasn't quite so bad, as day broke at 4 a.m. But winter with the wind howling around the corners and neighbours dying left and right made ghosts as plentiful as politicians. You just had to forget about enjoying yourself the night before you were supposed to get up. It was constantly on your nerves.

The Day Dida Died
Billy was another one who wasn't much help with the ghost situation. He would run into another room without telling you and holler back, "That place is lousy with ghosts," and then add, "Don't be scared, they'll only pull you in and hold you."

The thing about ghosts was that they didn't bother me much during the daytime. I was brave then, but at night —watch out.

One such instance was when this old Englishman, who I used to imitate all the time, died. We used to say to him, "It's a

98

nice day." And he would say "Dida". I don't know what Dida meant but it was sure fun mimicking him. The day he died I had been copying him all day and Billy said, "You'll be sorry when night comes, the way you're carrying on now." I laughed this off.

Night wore on and Murray, my bedmate at this time, was out late, so I went to bed when the rest did and was left alone to think about old Bob White and his "Dida".

I never sweat so much in my life as that night. I didn't know where to look. There were two windows and a big clothes closet that I couldn't look at. I was bound to see his face at the windows and if he wasn't there he would surely be in the closet. I didn't dare let my arm hang over the edge of the bed for fear a hand would reach out and pull me under. Finally, I went to sleep in a drip of sweat, with visions of Bob White dancing through my mind.

I didn't hear Murray sneaking in. It was very cold out that night. He had worn no mitts, and as he reached under the covers to see if I was under the right blanket (I had a knack for getting under the wrong one), icy fingers touched my leg. I snapped awake convinced that Bob White was not only in the room with me, but also in the bed. My low moan ascended to a blood curdling scream and sent Murray crashing out of the room and down the hall. We woke everybody in the house. Naturally, with everyone else awake I got very brave, and slipped off to sleep.

Out We Go Again

One dark dreary night in early fall, Pa was away to another meeting. There was no switch to turn off the kitchen light before retiring, so the last one to go to bed had to jump really high and, if luck was with you, catch the small beaded chain that hung from the socket. This jump came after all the other kids had passed the front room door and were on the curve to the stairs. It meant the one left to pull the chain had more power behind him than the blast off in the moon shots.

On this particular night, Pearl ran a little ahead of us to bed.

Not letting anyone know what she was up to, she stuffed herself under the blankets on Ma's bed and remained perfectly still as we assembled our clothes for the night.

All of a sudden, Teedy's large eyes bulged, looking at the human form under the covers; he wasn't long passing the word to the rest of us almost naked brothers shouting, "My God, there's someone in Ma's bed." Immediately a fierce marathon was in progress with Teedy leading the pack. Down the stairs and over to the neighbour's we ran in single file, necks straight out. Half way over we were interrupted by a loud wailing. It was Pearl crying hysterically, running behind us, and telling us through whimpers that it was her in the bed trying to fool us.

Embarrassed and undressed, we all walked back to the lonely house; and no more tricks of this nature were ever played by Pearl, who made it a point to be well in the rear on the way to bed.

The Night Billy Burglarized Pa

We not only had trouble with ghosts, but also one time with a burglar, who just happened to be a member of our family.

As Billy reached his late teens, he had a tendency to keep late hours. Pa never got wind of his escapades until one muggy summer night when Billy was eighteen. All the doors were locked for the night and everyone was asleep. Billy was my bedmate at this time. About 3 a.m. I was awakened by a commotion outside the window – somebody was out there waving his arms around. While I was still gazing sleepily out the window, Pa and Freddy came into the room. If there had been a light in our room, we would have noticed that Billy's side of the bed was empty. Instead, Pa, seeing the person outside flaying wildly with his arms, gave me a vicious shove saying, "Lay down or you'll be shot. There's a fool down there and he's pointing a gun at you." Hurriedly they left my room, Pa picking up our alarm clock in his flight to catch the maniac.

Billy told me later that he saw so many heads at the window, he decided he'd better get out of there and went around to get in the front room window. As he pushed open the window and climbed in, he knocked over a flower pot. Upstairs, Freddy whispered to Pa, "He's in the house," and the suspense built. Freddy, creeping behind Pa, grasped a claw hammer and Pa, with muscles taut, clutched the alarm clock.

The phone at the bottom of the stairs had two silver bells. As they rounded the top of the stairs, something glinted off the bells. "There he is," shouted Pa and sent the alarm clock reeling through the air, smashing the phone to pieces. Hearing this excitement, I began to realize Billy wasn't beside me in bed. I ran out and told Pa, "It's Billy." My father walked straight back to his room saying, "I'll deal with him in the morning." The sentence was that Billy had to go to bed when he got home from school for a whole month. Freddy, forty years later, is still ashamed to talk about the incident, but remembers he once had a job as a night watchman where his only means of protection was a hammer. Which was nothing compared with the other watchman who was armed only with an alarm clock.

The Bouncy Walk
Once in a while, Billy would invite me along on one of his escapades. I often made out none too well, and once the most exciting part of my evening was that I stepped on a ghost.

Considering ourselves sex symbols, we'd scrub ourselves to the bone –with great expectations of love from the opposite sex. But the clothes we had to wear didn't do much for our very clean bodies.

The clothes weren't dirty in any way because if Pa came close to you and breathed in your aura, he would charge you with not smelling right. Of course, most of the time we wouldn't huddle too close to Pa anyway as the touch of Pa to your body never had that buzzing feeling you'd get touching a young girl your age.

Billy got dressed for the dance to see his beautiful dream girl. He had on Pa's shirt, size 17 collar and Bill only took size 14, but at least it was a shirt; Pa's tie, so wide it could easily act as a vest; pants size 46 up under his chin. The coat was arranged so that no protrusions were showing.

Billy would never refuse any type of clothing. He was given a pair of spats by our older brother, Freddy. Starting new styles was right up his alley.

With Bill's shoes already in the shoemaker's getting half-soled, his sneakers had to match his garb. Luckily they were black and Bill wore them along with his grey spats. He looked like something you'd see coming up the Niagara Gorge to do some tedious tight-rope walking. Knowing what views of his feet would be seen, he'd place his feet at the proper angle making the sneaker look like a shoe. With the tight wrapping of the spat, it made him look even dressier, and his fans swarmed around him.

Knowing it was useless for me to try to get the girls to chase me with the garments I was wearing, I would have been better off had I stayed home, especially with what awaited me on the way back.

Anyway, not far from the girl's house, Bill called me aside to tell me he was going in to meet her. It was then 9 p.m.

"I'll wait for you here, if you're not too long," I told Bill. It was a long hike home, and Bill would be telling me of his advancements, etc., and so I'd wait.

I ended up waiting for him until 1 a.m., not knowing he had taken another route home. Streets were deserted, and I had no money for the five-cent bus ride; cars were almost extinct. My thoughts were not only on the three-mile hike, but also on three graveyards two miles ahead on the right side of the road.

To make it spookier, they had arranged those cemeteries on a bleak bank running a quarter of a mile along steep cliffs.

Something that the kids used to say kept running through my mind. They'd say, if you're passing this graveyard on a dark night (couldn't be any darker) and if you looked towards the centre of the graveyard, one tombstone that belonged to a rich undertaker would light up. Some phosphorus in the making was the reason.

Knowing exactly where it was, my subconscious hammered every step not to look at it. On the left of the graveyards, the sidewalks were very narrow and unpaved, and you had to walk carefully so that you wouldn't hit a stone with your sneakered foot. No lights on the hydro poles; all houses in darkness.

Five more minutes and I'd be in the heart of the graveyards. I think the Devil himself took over then. I know God wouldn't have done such a trick. My eyes were searching and scanning the many stones, then the lighted one appeared in my vision.

At this time I was stepping quite high as I didn't want to stub my toe. Trying to avert my head from looking in the direction of the tombstone, I walked full length along the body of a Newfoundland dog that was sleeping stretched out on the small path. Sleepy groans broke the silence with my every step.

It seemed as though someone had clasped a steel band on my head and tightened it. The last step was the dog's tail and with only about a mile to do, I must have flown the distance because at times I'd put my foot down and not hit bottom. Through the door, up the stairs, and smash right in the centre of my brothers, clothes still on.

After the band was released from my head, I got up after waking the others, undressed, told them my experience, checked my sneaker wound, moved a few legs here and there, and finally fit in like a sardine next to their snoring voices.

Lunch Time At the Wakes

With our fear of ghosts, you'd have thought we would have avoided wakes like the plague. But wakes had something we would battle even ghosts for – food.

At the wakes, family and friends would sit in the parlour with the body throughout the long evening, talking and sometimes joking until about midnight. Then everyone would go out into the kitchen for a meal, which consisted of food sent in by neighbours to help in this time of bereavement.

Once we had eaten, we would take up our vigil again until

the early morning, when we would trudge sleepily home and go to bed for the day so that we could come back the next night for another free meal. This would go on for three or four days.

This worked out well as long as we knew the person who had died, but often in the winter after a long skating session, we would attend wakes of people we didn't know from Adam, just to get that food.

The rink in Sydney Mines would have skating sessions – twenty-five cents for fifteen bands. If we couldn't whip up the twenty-five cents each, we'd often hitchhike to North Sydney to skate where the admission was only fifteen cents to outsiders. After skating and acting handsome for the girls for fifteen bands, no matter how tired and hungry we were, we'd still have to hitchhike or walk the three miles home.

We had tremendous appetites after all that skating, and about six of us would pool our resources and buy a five-cent paper. The latest events of the world weren't on our minds. Instead, we would turn to the obituaries, as it was almost midday. Lunch time at the wakes. We'd have enough sense to pick out a good street and a nice home, and usually a deceased male – as it's only proper the female be left (God help her) to muscle up the lunches. Not knowing the deceased, in fact never having seen any of the family, we found at a time like this there was no discrimination. We'd head for the house, skates on our weary shoulders. Then before we went in to offer our sympathies, we'd hide our skates under the porch step. The cap would come off in the left hand so that we could keep the right hand free to give that touch of sympathy.

We were led to the front room where the body was laid and would try to go through this ritual we had concocted in order to get in on the eating. We would walk single file – which was better than facing your brother or friend on that solemn occasion, as everyone of us would be on the verge of hysterical laughter. If it had happened, not only would we have been disgraced, but also we would have starved.

One of us would say, "He was a lovely man," with the bereaved wife chipping in saying, "He never hurt anyone." That was when it was hard to suppress the laugh because we all had the same thought – that if he came to she'd soon know six he'd hurt because he had never laid eyes on us. We'd make sure we got all the details from the paper before going in. Another one of us would pipe up saying, "He worked quite a while at the foundry."

"Oh yes, he was there for thirty years."

"Is his brother Jade coming home from Louisiana?"

"Oh yes, he'll be here tomorrow."

Our wicked bunch would soon get restless, but she would understand, thinking the death was quite a blow to us, which it was as we were almost fainting from suppressed laughter.

Another arrangement we had talked over before going in was in case she asked, "Would you care to eat?" We had appointed one of us to answer in a low, solemn tone, having been caught so many times before with all of us saying "OK" together, which never sounded right.

Then she'd lead us all to a dining-room. In the centre is the big table, sides up and the chairs in the right place. The table is loaded with food. We've passed initiation – our troubles are over and we've won our prize.

It was an advantage to us also when the mourners didn't eat at the table with us, as we were caused no embarrassment when reaching for our fifth piece of cake.

It was sad, but our presence was a lift to the mourners, even though we were there only on a starvation mission. Before leaving, we were so sincere with the mourners, they were inviting us back to the next wake. We could hardly keep from asking, "What's on the menu?"

One of my last trips to a wake was with the little lame pal of mine called Ducky, who had one leg much shorter than the other.

We entered the front door and the wife led us to the body in the parlour. We were alone then, as she retired to the kitchen. Looking the old man over, Ducky and I were discussing in a low voice the old saying that if you put your hand on their foreheads, you'd never forget them.

I reached over first and touched his forehead. Ducky, much shorter than me, leaned on his long leg and put too much pressure on the old man's head. At that second, the glue parted from the corpse's lips making a loud sucking noise. We made a frantic dash for the door with Ducky in the lead and reached home in record time.

At least we proved the old saying about touching foreheads. We'll never forget that old man if we live to be two hundred.

The Delicious Pound Party

Pound parties were invented just at the proper time for us brothers as no money was involved. All you had to do was take a pound of anything from butter to tea to the home having the party and drop it in the wicker basket near the door on your arrival. Each donation was well wrapped, and no one knew what the other had given. This pound of whatever was your entry fee and entitled you to stay for the dance and partake of a light lunch before the evening broke up. This was right up our alley.

Pa would buy P & G and Surprise soap from the co-operative by the case. It contained about a hundred bars, retailed at four cents, and by buying it in lots it would cost three cents a pound.

The best part of having those cases of soap was when a pound party was involved; usually it was a house party. We took a pound of soap, wrapped it in brown paper, and tied it up neatly. As you went in the house, there was a large clothes basket on the table. You threw your pound of whatever you had in the basket with the rest of the whatevers. The guilty look on your face hinted that you never put a pound of butter or tea in, but at least it was a pound.

In went the four of us. This cost us about twelve cents, and so we weren't going to leave until the sandwiches were all eaten, as we were legally in there like the rest.

There would usually be some old man on the fiddle and a

young boy on the guitar supplying the music for the night. No good dancers amongst us, we would sit back on an old chesterfield and watch the oldsters shuffle their bustles.

One summer evening, very damp and humid, after dropping the P & G soap in the basket, we noticed the mosquitoes had taken over the residence. There must have been millions in the kitchen where we were sitting – the back door wide open, the windows open, and not a screen. After twenty guests had arrived, all donating to the basket, the mosquitoes seemed to come in droves. You just couldn't stand the torture, and so the only thing to do was to get out.

The woman of the house hated to see us go but she knew that we couldn't carry on like this. So she suggested we just reach in on our way out and pick our pound and she would have the party the next cool night. I reached in to get mine and was satisfied with my grab, making sure I avoided the soap. We had to walk three miles and we had had no lunch there: only a few mosquitoes that had flown into our mouths as we were jabbering.

My package contained a pound of dates and Murray had a pound of cheese, more appetizing than two pounds of P & G soap. So we enjoyed the trip home that night. We walked every step of the way, our feet tired, but our stomachs happy from the choice mixture of cheese and dates.

Eating Again?

Every so often our greedy eating habits caused us some embarrassment.

In my heyday, hoboing was done more than hitchhiking. A few people had cars but would never pick anyone up. One warm summer's day, Billy and I hopped a freight, thinking we'd like to see more of the world. We had gone about ninety miles when we decided we couldn't stand the sound of steel hitting steel any longer.

Two in the morning, off we hopped and went into the roundhouse to sleep until morning. Sitting on a wooden bench with no back, Billy kept weaving back and forth until finally he fell right back on his head.

Knowing we couldn't go any further as we never had a penny and just couldn't miss any more sleep, we thought we'd try to hitchhike.

Billy and I had a hunger spell coming on. We decided to try the next house for a free meal. It was 5 p.m. and I wasn't lying when I told the lady we hadn't eaten all day.

Not having too much themselves, she said she'd get us a cheese sandwich and tea. But one sandwich only made us hungrier than we had been before going in. The only thing to do was to keep walking until we were out of sight of the house we had just eaten in and look for another before dark. Cream tartar biscuits and molasses was the meal we received in the next house.

Houses in the country were sometimes miles apart. We continued walking along the not-too-busy highway, now 10 p.m., and stomach thinking the throat was cut, when we saw a lighted farmhouse. It was Bill's turn to see what meal we could get. Entering the gate, we waited as I rapped a second time. "Who is there, what do you want?" came the hurried question. Telling him our mission, a man opened the door and listened to our hungry plea: the same old line that we hadn't eaten since morning. "There's not much here, but it will help you over the night."

It was bulky food, just what we wanted: homemade bread, corn beef and potatoes – a real down-to-earth meal. We stuffed our stomachs tightly before leaving for the long walk. We had walked so many miles that our legs were beginning to hop up, as though we had no control over them, even when we stopped.

We decided to ask if we could stay for the night. But before we got out the question, "Could we sleep here for the night?" the man said, "I'm sorry there's no place to put you up for the night here." So we depended on the next house to put us up at this late hour. Filled up and feeling much better, I still had a craving for something sweet, not having had any dessert with the big meal we had just put away. On we marched down the unlighted road. After a half hour or so from the big supper, I motioned to Bill that there was a weak light in the distance.

Strawberry jam, homemade bread, and hot tea was our meal, after our sad story of not eating since early morning. It sure tasted good after the walk from the last house.

Radios were scarce in the countryside. Some people would come for miles to listen to the sometimes fifteen-round championship fights over the small battery radio. This very night we found out one was to be broadcast at eleven p.m.

After a deep conversation with us about our adventures, the three elderly people were all ears listening to the rounds of boxing. Sitting at the table, swabbing the strawberry jam on the freshly cut bread, we felt as though we had known these people for years. Suddenly we heard footsteps, then a dog's bark. The same door we had entered about forty minutes ago was now filled with the stalwart frame of the man in the last house, where we had eaten heartily for an hour. This visiting farmer had come all the way down to hear the fight on the other fellow's radio. Looking directly at us, he said, "Eating again?" The man said to the visitor, "You don't know these boys, do you?" "Well they just ate at my house, not more than an hour ago," was the answer. We were embarrassed, but we never knew which one of the food-givers to be embarrassed to.

We did have a little pride. Thanking him for his trouble, we red-facedly walked out the gate, not saying anything to each other yet, as we were still close to the house.

Feet red-hot and no end in sight, I told Bill we'd have to go some place, even if we had to sleep on a roof. Luck was with us as I saw a lamp in a window. Rushing up before the lamp went out, I gave a loud rap. An elderly man, two sons, and a daughter all poked heads at us at once. They were a poor family; we could tell by the furniture and the size of the house. This was our last chance, the morning was slipping by. We'd find it hard to find a house if it wasn't lit up. Our story was we had no place to stay and couldn't walk – our legs were beat. "Is there any place we could sleep, even on the floor?" The old man grabbed at his heavy moustache and looked towards the floor, ready to speak. "My wife died a few days ago and the mattress she died on is in the shed out back. You fellers could sleep on that. I'll light the lantern, so you can find your way up the loft to the mattress." This sounded good as we were too tired to be scared.

After getting us set up in the loft, he warned us not to leave the lantern burning, as he was saving on oil. We agreed everything would be taken care of. The odour from the old mattress was so strong that we had to take our shirts off and tie them around our noses. The only thing we removed besides our shirts was our boots. Bill said we were quite close to a railroad as he could hear train whistles and that if he heard a freight come, he was going to rush down and hop it.

If I woke up and found myself alone, I knew I'd die with fright. So I sneakily hid one of Bill's shoes in a good spot before going to sleep; and as the long freight was passing, Bill was struggling looking for his other shoe.

Nine

All For One and One For All

Tobacco Pudding Clubhouse
In the winter it got quite boring in Sydney Mines as there was
no place we could meet with our buddies.

With this in mind, one of our friends came up with a good
idea: "Let's start a clubhouse." His mother, being overly protective and wanting her son near her, said we could use their
cellar. Her only worry was that since there were no lights in
the cellar we would have to be careful if she gave us a kerosene lamp. We assured her we had lamps at our house and
there was nothing she could warn us about lamps that we
didn't already know.

Pa, besides being a tobacco chewer, was also an ardent pipe
smoker. (He never smoked cigarettes, and if he'd ever caught
us with one, it would have been the same as being caught
with heroin; so we made a point of smoking the whole cigarette so as not to have any butts lying around.)

He bought his pipe tobacco by the case. Not thinking we
would smoke a pipe, he would leave the whole box exposed in
the back porch.

About ten of us went to our clubhouse this night, an ideal
night for us as Pa had gone to a meeting. Bill got three of Pa's
pipes and four plugs of his Bangor tobacco.

Our friend's mother was rather feeble and couldn't get
down to the cellar to see if her only son was enjoying himself.

111

His father was working on night shift, and so we had it made.

Every now and then his mother would call him from the top of the stair, asking was he warm, etc. This being the first night we had to be careful, and so we treated her son well or else we would have been out in the cold. Three of us took one of Pa's pipes and as fast as Bill stripped pieces off the plug tobacco with the scissors, they were jammed in the big bowls of the pipes. Our friend wanted to have one of the pipes to smoke, but as three were already enjoying them, he'd have to wait.

Another call came down from the worried mother to see if her son wanted another sweater on. Bill kept tearing off the tobacco. Then turning the tobacco box over, he read on the side that it was good to chew also. Our friend's ears flew up, and he said he'd sooner chew than smoke, as that was all his uncle ever did and it wasn't as hard on your heart.

Bill quickly passed him an inch square of the plug, reminding him not to bite on it – to just suck it and it wouldn't go to pieces. Now everyone who was pipeless had a wad in his mouth, spitting steadily into an old bean can.

We were used to chewing it as Pa had been trusting and had left it around for years, so that we could almost chew like Pa, only we couldn't hit a cuspidor like he could.

The mother calls again about whether it was too cold down there, and if so for her son to come up. Her boy answered her in a gurgling fashion, rolling the wad clockwise in his mouth so that she could make out his words.

Jokes were then the highlight; and as we chewed and spit, each one tried to tell the funniest yarn. We began to notice that her son was turning the colour of porridge. The rest of us knew he was in labour and proceeded to do something about it. Although we were in a semi-drunken state ourselves, we had sense enough to try and look after him.

He still pushed the big chew around with his tongue, not thinking to spit it out. We kept the jokes flying, trying to take his mind off his condition, when one kid in a fit of laughter after a hilarious joke hit our friend on the back with such a whomp that sonny boy gagged and swallowed the whole chew. His colour changed to a dull grey. We made for him and thumped him on the back.

All chews were spit out in the bean can. The son was moaning and drunk. "What should we do?" There was no safety exit. We'd have to pass his mother if she didn't pass out when she saw him. He had enough strength to tell us to blow out the light. We proceeded up the cellar stairs. His mother grabbed him and led him to the sofa saying, "I might have known the smell of the kerosene in that dingy cellar would make you sick."

Just then he gave a loud burp and heaved up the wad. We watched the evidence hit the basin. Seeing this chaw come up, she said, "That blood pudding you had for supper, mind the last time you ate it, you got real sick."

We knew this would be our last meeting at this hang-out, as his mother knew he was allergic to kerosene lamps and blood pudding. Bill still had a plug of tobacco left from the four we had brought, and so we journeyed down the street to our homes with a brand new chew that had to be spit out before we entered home. Then came intensive gargling so that we could appear before Pa with sweet-smelling breath.

Eat, Drink, and Be Mousey
If Pa had ever caught us smoking, we wouldn't be around today. But if he had ever seen us drinking, he wouldn't even have allowed us to be reincarnated after he'd killed us. He was a teetotaler. Everything alcoholic was banned from the house. Relatives visiting knew Pa's orders. "Come in, but leave your bottle outside." We soon caught on to this and would grab the relative's bottle and head for the shore. Nothing would be said to Pa by the relative as he didn't want to let on to Pa he even had a bottle.

Never having any money, this seemed the only way we could get a drink until a friend came up with a recipe for blackberry wine and we decided to make our own home brew.

We had a secret meeting at our place one night when Pa was away. Where were we to set the brew? After some discussion, we all volunteered to meet at our place to concoct the brew –four brothers and four friends in on the deal. The night picked for this hazardous job was most important. It would have to be the night Pa was at his lodge meeting from eight till ten. Dividing up the recipe was next on the agenda. Each friend vowed he'd bring an ingredient and we would get the berries.

The night came and everybody was Johnny-on-the-spot. Bill, being the houselady at the time, came in with an old bread pan we could afford to do without in our daily chores.

The berries, raisins, yeast, prunes, sugar, and things that weren't even called for were thrown in the old bread pan. A friend heard an old man had thrown in a fig of tobacco, so in one went at Pa's expense.

Now for a place to let it set for three weeks. Bill soon fathomed that one out: an old icebox in the porch was the ideal spot. A pan placed under the icebox to catch the drippings was removed. This was corrected to suit our need by placing a piece of garden hose on the outlet, then drilling a hole through the floor, allowing the water from the ice to drip through under the porch. Now we had space to put our brew mixture. Sliding the heavy pan with contents under was performed by Bill, without a spill.

After about ten days, you would have thought we had a watch dog. Coming in the porch from outside, you could hear weird growling sounds coming from the direction of the old icebox. It got louder and louder each day.

In order to keep Pa from hearing it, there was one of three things we'd have to do: one, strangle Pa; two, disconnect the porch from the house; or three, remove the powerful liquor from the porch to the shore.

Three more days before it was ready and just an hour before Pa got home, we got our bottles and corks ready for the bottling. Shades in the kitchen were lowered and the front and back doors locked. The Mounties would be interested in this find as well as Pa. Bill proceeded to pull the noisy mixture from under the icebox and set it on the table. Everyone was at their happiest.

The berries had swelled in size and covered the top of the mixture. Murray with recipe in hand read off the instructions. Marley (a dear friend who derived his name from the ghost in Dickens' *Christmas Carol* from me, years before) was voted to squeeze the juice from the berries: every drop. All mouths were watering with cups in hand for the testing. Marley reached in the pan and came up with both hands full of berries. As he squeezed, he gave a screech; his hands flew open, and he threw a wine-logged mouse against the wall, berries and all. All faces dropped at the sight as we placed our empty cups on the table. What a long wait for this disappointment! It wasn't long before we twigged how the mouse got into our brew. It had jumped up on the pan ledge which was a half inch from the icebox floor. But how long it had been floating there kept us guessing.

The swelled-up mouse was thrown into the coal stove. Pa would be home in less than an hour. Marley in a faint voice said he had heard where they used mice for medicines. Experiments probably, some of us figured he meant. But then again we were eager to believe anything. At the same time Marley dunked his cup into the mouse wine to lead the parade. We made no attempt to stop him and waited for the reaction.

Marley kept his colour and composure after the first cup, but a few minutes later went into a torrent of laughter and reaching for more, his frenzied laugh continued. It wasn't long before the rest of us got our cups and slopped them in the pan. "Drink up before Pa gets home," was Bill's command.

No bottling was done this night – the bottles were taken outside in a box and shoved under the porch. Just one big free-for-all taken right from the bread pan. It wasn't long before the pan was empty and the mouse forgotten. Ten minutes before Pa was to arrive the laughing hyenas left for home. After cleaning up as best we could, we staggered off to bed. Waking every hour with thoughts of mouse wine in our heavy heads, we asked ourselves, "Why did we drink it so greedily?", hoping Marley was right about the mouse medicine, as we needed all the doctoring we could get right about then.

The Skeleton's Last Stand

At fifteen, we really wanted to belong to Boy Scouts. They went camping for two weeks in the summer and how we would have loved to be free of Pa for that length of time. Usually just the rich were eligible to join, but Murray and I found out the Scouts were to have a bean supper to finance the camping trip. So Murray, who had the most gall, asked the minister if there was any chance he and I could join Scouts. The minister gave us a bunch of tickets to sell and said we could join the Scouts on one condition: that we were to serve at the supper the following Tuesday. Nothing could have been more delightful to us. Here we were, Boy Scouts, and we would be waiting on girls our age. We never gave a thought to the boys, mothers, or fathers; but the girls were on our minds continuously. The night before, we stayed up half the night brushing our teeth and trying to arrange a handsome smiling face for the occasion.

However, the next day things didn't go just the way we had expected. They caught us eating while we were serving, and Murray ruined the deacon's trousers while serving on a slant. But we were undaunted – we were so happy to be there and serving all those girls – until we began to notice people were evading us. They didn't seem to want us to give them their supper. This made us more nervous, and we tried to serve all the faster and became more careless.

We were almost starved ourselves, and we were trying to get the thing over with fast, so that we could relax. When it was finally over they tried to get Murray and me to do all the dishes alone. But we had had six years with dishes and a heavy schedule at home, and there was no organization,

Scouts or otherwise, that was going to bully us. So we did our share and left the rest for the doctors' and dentists' sons.

At each Scout meeting the Scout Master would line us up and ask each one of us to tell his good deed for the week. I would salute, step out, and tell him I had helped an old woman across the street with her parcels. I hadn't seen an old woman all week, let alone one with parcels, but that was my constant deed. Murray wouldn't use my deed. I'd hear him mumbling something about cleaning up some old man's yard. It was all I could do to keep from looking seriously at the Scout Master and saying, "Murray is a damn liar."

Then they would show you slip knots and how to survive after you'd been dead in the woods for two days. After this, they would escort about twelve of us into another room where an old Englishman, who was a first-aid man in the mines, would teach us first aid. It was almost impossible to make out his gibberish. I'm sure sometimes even he didn't know what he was talking about. If he found out you weren't listening to him, he'd shame the life out of you by saying, "If you listened more to things like this, you wouldn't be so skinny and miserable-looking." It was so boring we kept thinking, "Let's get the hell out of here."

The old man kept a skeleton, which closely resembled him, in a closet to teach us more about the human body. He loved that skeleton and must have told us fifty times it cost over a hundred dollars. At the meetings, the last half hour always ended in games. During a game of hide and seek at our last meeting, Murray and I happened to hide in the same closet, the one with the skeleton. It was on Murray's side of the closet when we entered. Boy, was it dark after we closed the door. Waiting there, not breathing so that no one would find us, I felt the skeleton's hand close around my neck. I took one deathly swipe at the beast and knocked it to the floor in a hundred pieces. We knew this was going to bring our Scout episode to an abrupt end. When the old man saw his prize gone forever, he started to cry. It was the first time we had seen an older person cry and we were amazed, not at how he felt, but at how he looked.

We were thrown out of the Scouts. That was our last bean supper, the last skeleton I ever swung at, and the last time I lied about helping an old woman with parcels across the street. They wanted our pins too, but we kept them.

Ten

Sex and the Single Tooth

Amy Took Ma's Trinkets to Boston
Murray and I, in Grade One, had this beautiful feeling for a
sweet little girl named Amy. She was the only thing that interested us. We thought of her night and day.

We never knew what theft meant at that age, but we in-
dulged in it. Everything Ma and our sisters dropped on the
table, pins, bracelets, or any shiny object, were picked up by
Murray and me and transported to Amy the next day in our
little black bags. How her big blue eyes, with the extra long
lashes, would flutter when one of us would give her Ma's best
beads.

Jealousy between Murray and me never existed; it was a
divided love. He gave her Ma's jewelry and I gave her our sisters' trinkets. She accepted everything with sweet little open
arms. If I'm not mistaken, I'm sure she wore a mini-skirt, but
the name mini wasn't applied then. I guess it was a change for
us to see legs as sweet as hers since the rest of the girls' legs
were bulked up with ribbed cotton socks, which contained
not only the legs, but rolls of spare long johns as well. We
never went for this style – the mini was our favourite.

We could always pick Amy out in a crowd. She wore one of
the sweetest blue sweater coats I ever saw. We were even interested in our own attire and tried to look our best.

They say there isn't such a thing as a broken heart, but after hearing the news about Amy, there were two of them. Her father came to get her from school one morning about an hour after we had marched in. They were moving to Boston, which was almost like going to China in our minds. Our oldest sister had gone to Boston, and she always seemed so far away. Oh, that sad day when she raised her little arm with sister's bracelet on it, bidding us goodbye. It was as though our world had gone. Our appetites lessened (just for a while). Telling Ma the story, we were cheered up a bit when she said, "Never mind, some day you can visit your sister in Boston and look her up." But by the time Murray and I got to Boston, it would be a miracle if we could pick her out in a crowd. She might still be wearing the little mini-skirt and that sweet blue sweater coat, but numerous other girls would probably be wearing the same outfit. I guess the only way we'd be able to recognize her would be by the jewelry we gave her, which had triggered the sweet smile from our dear little Amy.

Look Bill, No Teeth
With girls always on our mind, we had a lot of pride in our teeth.

We were constantly reminded by Pa and Ma to keep them in good shape. We all had our own toothbrush, which we were to hang on a nail when not in use. Salt and soda was our cheap tooth cleaner, and since out of eleven children, we all still have our own teeth, the solution we were using must have been good for the teeth, possibly better than toothpaste.

Billy and I at the age of seven had the same two front baby teeth. If you could call them teeth. They were a khaki colour in front and black as tar around the edges. But the roots were solid and a good tug wouldn't jar them. How we hated those teeth, especially when we had to talk to a girl. We did everything in our power to have them loosened, except have them pulled by the family doctor. We prayed each night for the Lord to loosen them, and first thing in the morning Bill would pull on his and I'd try mine for firmness, but it was no go. They were still there – what was left of them.

At school one day, because of the inclement weather the teacher decided we could play in the basement. In those days the cheapest form of horse to play with was your brother or a friend, provided you had the small piece of rope to go over his shoulders and under his arms. We had the same signals as for a real horse. When you pulled on the right side of the rope, he'd go to the right and even kick at you, if he'd had a good breakfast.

I happened to come from behind the girder and got in the path of one of the horses. The reins were level with my lip, the rope caught in my teeth and yanked out both my front teeth, a job a bulldozer would have had trouble with. The first thing I did was reach for my mouth and look at my hand to see if I was bleeding. I saw the blood and felt the vacancy and went into a frightened coma for a few minutes. Then I came to, to find the horse and driver had carried me up and placed me on the teacher's desk.

The attention I got that morning was astonishing. The teacher was so sympathetic. The kids acted as though I had been run over by a six-ton truck, but as soon as the blood stopped, the pity wore off. When I looked in the mirror and saw those two ugly teeth gone, even with empty gums, I thought I was one of the sexiest males in the school. I could hardly wait to see how envious Billy would be when I gave him my Colgate smile, with him still trying to lose his uglies.

There's a Tooth In My Egg

Our older sisters also imprinted it in our brain that our whole future, whether we got a job or a wife, depended on good-looking teeth.

Once I got a job doing gardening for the manager of a large store. For a sixty-hour week I was paid four dollars, which really helped as I needed some work done on my teeth.

One tooth being a shade longer in front than the other, I consulted a dentist, thinking all they'd have to do was file it even with the other tooth and cap it with gold around the edge. But once a dentist gets in your mouth with a needle, your face is in such bad shape they could transplant your nose and you wouldn't know it until the feeling came back.

After all his drilling and asking questions (why do they always ask questions and expect answers while four fingers, one thumb, and a pound of wool are jammed in your mouth?), he sat me up and gave me a mirror.

I would never have known myself. My good tooth had been cut away by three-quarters to a little pointed dot that didn't even resemble a tooth. I was furious. I thought of strangling the dentist. Then I thought of suicide. How could I face people with one of my teeth looking like the tooth on a sawblade? Really upset, and my face still needled, I then felt the dentist put something over the tooth. Passing me the mirror again, I wasn't as mad. A cap had been put over the stump and now the teeth were even. I was sort of embarrassed by the way I had acted when I first saw that whittled-away point of a tooth.

In the mood now to do less talking, I climbed out of the chair without asking any questions, feeling that what's done is done. The dentist said, "See you the twenty-sixth of the month." After I left, I wondered why the dentist wanted to see me again. I thought he had finished with me. (Maybe he had a part for me in a movie and was going to file *all* my teeth to a point so that I could play the part of the vampire.)

Easter week-end was not far off. The custom was to buy candied Easter eggs, coloured eggs, etc., much the same as is done today. The eggs were a gummy paste inside, the outside chocolate-covered. Being invited to a friend's house, I could hardly wait to get over there, as they had a new boarder, a school teacher. The word around town was that she was quite beautiful. With my tooth level with the other one and gleaming, I felt my charm would make me irresistible, and I planned to do as much laughing as possible.

Sitting around the table, the teacher, the mother, her son and I were having a light Easter lunch – candied eggs cut in slices, served with hot tea. Putting all my masculine abilities into a story I was telling, with everyone interested and waiting for the exciting climax – I felt an air pocket and a vacancy during the swishing of my tongue. Good Lord, my front tooth is out –I made a mad dash for the bathroom, not even pardoning myself or telling them what had happened. In the bathroom, with my mouth still gummed up from the egg, I took a look in the mirror and saw a dirty vacancy right where the white cap had dressed up that ugly peg moments before. Rolling the gummed mixture out on my hand, I began searching for my cap, trying to salvage it so I could place it back on the peg and finish my interesting story that had ended so suddenly. Pressing together a bulk piece of the candy, I could see the shape of the cap; I was surprised it hadn't been crushed. Latching on to it, I proceeded to clean it up.

Downstairs I came, the cap on very loosely. I hardly dared breathe let alone think of finishing the half-told story. Everyone was waiting to know what had happened. The mother asked, "Why did you leave in such a rush?" I replied, "I felt like I was going to have a bad spell." (Which I almost did.) Everyone being somewhat concerned about my well-being, they didn't press me to finish the story, which made me feel very relieved. I soon left and rushed to the phone, getting the dentist out of bed as by now it was 10 p.m. I began telling him about the cap he'd just put on that day, how he'd over-charged me, and most of all what terrible embarrassment it had caused me. I blubbered on not giving him a chance to defend himself.

"Sorry, sir, for all this inconvenience, but that's only a temporary cap until we make the original in a few days," said the dentist. Why hadn't I listened to him as I was getting out of the chair?

Why dentists don't give a person a spare cap while waiting for the permanent gets me, as so many things can happen. For instance, one time I was boarding a local bus. It was midnight and I was sitting in one of those double seats that face each other, when two pretty girls got on and occupied the seat facing me. Riders were few at this hour. The driver made his way towards the highway. Everything was quiet as we drove through the sleepy morning.

I was never subject to sneezing, but I suddenly came forth, without warning or preparation, with a violent sneeze. Luckily, I saw this white object flying through the air in the girls' direction landing beneath their legs.

It wasn't noticed by anyone and I was glad of that. After thrusting my tongue in the huge gap in the front of my mouth, I just knew I had to get that cap fast. Spying it beneath their legs, I made a quick lunge among those legs to retrieve the cap. Screaming hysterically, the girls thought I had turned into a sex maniac.

Once back in my seat with a good grip on the cap, the girls calmed down, but the bus driver, taken aback by the girls' screams, brought the bus to a near crawl. Knowing he wanted to know about what had just happened, I bent over his shoulder and told him in a whisper. Quite humorous himself, it wasn't hard for him to understand the predicament I had been in.

Three or more miles up the road the girls got off, staring at me until they disembarked as though I were some kind of weirdo.

I Was a Painted Bag
Billy not only took great care of his teeth, but was also always the dressy one, even at Hallowe'en. He'd dress as a clean-cut, good-looking young man on the outside, but if you were to take him apart, you'd find Pearl's long looked-for sweater for underwear, pinned at the waist with his legs comfortably through the arms. This undergarment was worn not just at Hallowe'en, but also throughout the year. But there was no doubt about it, outside he was a dream to look at.

With all the girls in our family, my costume would be a dress. I'd have a false face and as breathing was restricted, possibly because of a tight bra or drawers, I would cut or bite a big piece out for the mouth. I can still taste the painted mouth of the false face.

At this time Billy was interested in the dentist's daughter, who would have put the prettiest movie star to shame. She was an angel and she loved Billy. The rest of us boys loved her more than Bill ever could, but that's as far as we got. I was very bashful around her and only once spoke to her. She sat in front of me in school, and one day she turned around and asked me a question. Well, that was too much. All the hidden love I had for her overcame me, and when I started to answer I stuttered, which I wasn't accustomed to doing. I couldn't get the answer out fast enough, and I ended up spraying her with spit so badly she reached for her lily white hanky with a disgusted look on her face and renewed her original position, with me still suffering the answer.

She lived three miles from our home. Bill was quite nervous this Hallowe'en about passing through the dark wood between our house and hers, and so he coaxed me to go with him. It was quite cold, about thirty degrees, and I don't know why I didn't dress more warmly. I guess I hoped she might take a very bad spell and fall for me, and so I didn't wear anything too bulky. I made my bosom out of a pair of Pa's long johns that were waiting to be washed (that was enough right there to lose her love), and to hold the bosom I used a sweater tied with a string. I put on one of my sister's skirts and a pair of panties and that was the extent of my costume. I figured we would be walking fast, and I would warm up. I really should have put on my long johns to act as a ballast. Anyway, we began our journey. I was a painted bag, trying to seduce my good looking brother.

We arrived at her house in an hour or so, and I can still see the sweet smile she gave Billy, who was maskless. When she looked at me with my mouth-bitten false face and one bosom much lower than the other, she gave me the same look I had received from her in school the day I smothered her with spit. I knew I wasn't wanted, but I had to stay and escort Billy back again through the woods. Someone suggested we have a game of hide and seek. So outside we went to a little area of trees she had around her house. There were three other couples. I was the only single, what you'd call a Baggy Butler. But I was invited to play too.

After a couple of good hides, the coming out and trying to blend in with the couples was rough going on me. So I thought, "I know what I'll do. I'll hide so well, no one will be able to find me until it's time to go home." Still sporting my skirt, I picked a good spot about fifteen feet up a tree. It required both arms to hold on, when all of a sudden – zip – Pearl's skimpy drawers fell off and landed on a branch about ten feet down the tree. I was a perfect specimen for *Playgirl* magazine, but you had to look up the tree to get the best results. Meanwhile, down at the bottom of the tree looking up was the dentist's daughter. My thoughts were, "If I let go, I'll land right on her head, and if I go higher, I'll never reach Pearl's drawers." I didn't breathe or move and either the Lord was good and she didn't see me, or else she was too embarrassed to speak, because she left and went further on.

I came down the tree like an orangutang, clutching the silk drawers in my hand. I made a dash for Billy, and said, "Look!" I opened my hand and they flew right in his face.

I was glad I never had to wear those flimsy articles on my body again.

Six Cents, Just To See the Back of Her Head
Now why couldn't I be as bold as Billy when it came to expressing my affections for a girl? I loved one girl for years without anyone ever knowing, not even my best friend.

She lived over two miles from me and yet I knew almost every move she made, where she was visiting, etc. I'd meet her on the street but never look directly at her. I'd continue past with a burning love in my heart wishing I had the guts to say, "Hello there, how are you, and where are you going?"

Here I was on my way to the show again, taking a different route than Pa coming home from work. I began to think of my mystery girl. The show was in progress when I got there and with only the light from the movie screen, my eyes wandered around the theatre over different shaped heads and hats to finally come to rest on Marion's. She – interested only in the picture; me – interested only in her. I sat right behind her, listening to every sigh and drinking in every toss of her head – six cents every week just to watch the back of Marion's head.

In school Murray would joke and play with her not knowing I was seriously jealous of him. Billy would talk to her and hug her as though she were his sister, and how easily she could have been Billy's girlfriend because he wasn't the least bit shy.

Dreams of her were heaven, until I awoke and found myself tangled up with my brother's legs.

When other fellows would start talking about her, I was always ready with a lie, saying, "Her sister is much prettier," though I knew she had no sister, or, "She has a boyfriend anyway." This seemed to work at times – at least they'd talk about someone else.

My friendship towards her two brothers in school was better than with my other friends. If they had been members of the Mafia, I would still have done anything for them just because they were related to her.

One day one of them asked me if I wanted to buy a pair of skates. Glancing down at his foot, I could see he wore at least three sizes larger than me, but if he'd had Giant McCaskill's foot it wouldn't have stopped the sale. He wanted two dollars for the skates. I would have been willing to pay twenty.

Having sold five dollars worth of iron and scrap for two dollars, I went to his house to pick up the skates, with thoughts that I might see Marion and that this might be the turning point in our love.

There she was in the living-room studying her lessons. She never noticed me. Her brother told me to try the skates on for size, but I assured him they would fit and struggled to get out of there as my heart was bursting with love.

One twenty-below-zero day in January, Stooky, the fellow next door, who was also in love but with a different girl, asked me if I would accompany him to the big pond where his girlfriend usually went skating.

It was five miles from home and ordinarily I would have said no on such a cold day, but I had half a smile on my face knowing what Stooky didn't, that on the way we'd pass Marion's house.

It had rained recently and the streets were a sheet of ice, and so we decided to skate there. This was good for Stooky's act. Now he could skate right into his sweetheart's arms like a handsome knight in armour.

Two miles on our way, we almost froze to death against a forty-mile-an-hour wind, but stubborn and determined, we never gave up the battle. I warmed considerably as I passed Marion's house, taking three quick peeks, only to find every window thick with frost. When we reached our destination, tired and frozen, the large pond was crackling with frost and small gusts of snow raced across the ice. But there was not a soul in sight. Stooky was heartbroken, but I wasn't too disappointed as I was thinking of Marion's house on the return trip.

Starting back, Stooky was crying with the cold, but I was holding my own at least until I had passed Marion's place. Arriving home, we pretended we had enjoyed our venture, making it sound very exciting, when in fact we had nearly frozen to death, our legs almost paralyzed from the ten-mile run over patches of dirt and ice. Just so Stooky could see his precious love and me take my lover's peek.

Free Burlesque

Sex wasn't shown in the theatres like it is today, but that never limited our sexual activities. We learned the hard way and enjoyed every second. A warm summer's evening would find our bunch sitting around telling adventures witnessed from the night before. Sometimes it would run into the wee hours.

Across from where we hung out lived a beautiful, shapely brunette, who could make any male's heart skip a beat. Billy always knew where she was that night, the exact time she'd be undressing for bed, and in which bedroom.

One street light on the corner a few feet from our house

guided the brunette into her house. But it made viewing difficult, and so its life was soon snuffed out by a crack-shot stone-thrower. The darkness made us more at ease.

There we were, twenty peepers waiting and watching for that perfect scene when the light in the window would go on and the strip tease would begin. The seat space you occupied before the light went on was where you were to sit. There was no moving around allowed once the show was on. You had to keep perfectly still.

A rich old man across the way, with a belly like a poisoned pup and a very nosey wife, would wonder what our game was. He was forever phoning the police at the least murmur.

This joyous peeping went on for the whole summer, and we all seemed to be thriving on it. When we wanted to know where our brunette was, the fellows would say, "Where's Bill?" and sure enough, he'd know her whereabouts and would advise us of the proper time to pick our seats.

Tall maple trees were behind us, their strong limbs and large leaves shading us so that even a rainy evening in summer didn't interfere with our peering. We would all be there, breathing heavily and waiting for that snap of the switch.

We were all bonded not to tell any outsiders, as we wanted this to be a secret. If it got around town they'd brand us as sex maniacs and peeping toms – and some would be jealous.

One night old beer-belly and his wife began snooping out their window from across the street. We knew where his phone was and, through a dim light in the window, watched his shadowy form proceed towards it. There were only two ways the police could come, and we all went wall-eyed keeping watch and peeping at the same time.

Every heart was beating its normal thump as the light had been delayed well beyond the appointed time prophesied by Bill. It was 1 a.m. and we were still waiting. Then came the bitter with the sweet. Brightness suddenly lit up the shadeless window at the same time the police cruiser stopped. Our pleasure was abruptly cancelled as we saw four police officers coming in our direction. In seconds there wasn't one kid on the ground, but the tree was suddenly populated with silent monkeys.

As usual, knowing our bunch the police gave no chase. Instead they turned sharply. Seeing what we had been watching, they became speechless and stood there in the same position as we had – in ecstasy.

Eleven

The Executioner and Jobs Jinx

The Strangled Rooster
During one of the Bunny Rabbit woman's visits, I became a murderer.

It was one dull winter's afternoon and having a tremendous appetite, I was disappointed to see what was on the menu. It wasn't hard to guess, seeing Bunny scrape the scales off three salt herring. I walked from the house and was astonished to see hens walking around the yard, as we had no hens ourselves.

There were twenty large hens, led by a Barred Rock rooster, strutting leisurely about. They had picked their way over from the home where Bunny had worked for years.

What a meal one of those would make! Not knowing the housekeeper's reaction to such a thought, I wondered how I could approach her with my idea.

Would she tell Pa or phone up the neighbour? Time was slipping by; it was now 2 p.m. Killed, cleaned, and cooked by 5 p.m.? Rushing into the house, I beckoned Bunny to look out at all the hens in the yard. She said, "That rooster would be good eatin' if a person could catch it."

"Do you think they'd miss it?" was my hasty question.

"'Oly smokes, no," she said in her Newfoundland brogue. That was what I had been waiting to hear.

Having never killed anything other than a mosquito, I was trying to get up the nerve to slaughter my prey. Maybe she knew a fast way to kill it, and so I went in for her advice. "Wring the bloody thing's neck," was her answer. That seemed much better than cutting its head off. I prepared for the kill. A piece of bread was broken up in little pieces and put in the path of the rooster. The path of broken bread led him right in through an open door to our old shed.

One more trip in to see Bunny: "How long would it take to cook him?" I asked in a guilty tone.

"About two 'ours in a 'ot hoven," she replied.

With the strut of an executioner, I walked towards the shed and opened the door. The rooster wasn't the least bit scared, just very friendly. This didn't help the situation as I was hoping it would at least be brazen or something. But no, it walked slowly around the shed picking a few hayseeds here and there. Sitting down on an old sofa and studying my victim, my eyes went to an old washtub hanging on the wall. After wringing its neck, I'd place it under the tub to muffle the noise.

On the floor beside me was a small axe, the blade about a half-inch thick at its sharpest point; it was then I thought, "Lucky I don't have to behead it, as that axe wouldn't cut a fly's wing." Preparing to muffle the racket, things were turning in my favour. A plane flew over the shed and that's when I grabbed my kidnapped friend and wrung its neck for two solid minutes. The sound of breaking bones sickened me. I threw it under the old washtub and departed for the house.

The housekeeper looked twice to make sure it was me. "Look in the mirror," she said. Besides shaking confusedly, I was snow white. After regaining my composure, I looked her in the eye saying, "That's the last time I'll ever attempt that. No matter how hungry I am, I'll eat fish."

"Pff, it's all over now," says she with a contented look. "Go get the beast and I'll 'ustle it in the 'oven".

Out I go for my victim. Raising the old tub, ready to grab

two stiff legs and gallop into Bunny, my blood curdled at the sight before me. There he was on his two legs, cawing and talking as friendly as before – except that his head was turned directly to the side and remained that way.

I wondered if he could live like that. Should I let him out? All these thoughts were driving me mad. Looking at the wide-bladed axe on the floor, I reached for it about the same time the rooster was making his rounds. Reaching out a strong arm, I grabbed the rooster, laid its head on the floor, and came down with every ounce of strength I had. I not only cut its head clean off but the dull axe also went into the floor two inches.

Taking the rooster by the warm legs, I carried it to Bunny and said, "Here, take this, I don't like chicken and I'm not even hungry." Even the lovely smell of the rooster cooking while I was resting didn't raise my appetite for chicken, and later on I fell back on my favourite dish: tea, bread, and molasses.

Follow the Flies
Always on the lookout for a good business venture, Billy and I happened to be on the wharf early in the morning one warm July day, when a fisherman came in with his big catch. We would be repaid by a string of fish if we helped him hold the boat or grab the tow-line. We needed money to see a Western show, and so Bill and I got our heads together. After the fisherman left, we looked at all those flapping fish left for lobster bait in the big oil drum. We decided to sell some to make a few pennies for the show.

Getting two wheels off an old carriage, we were now involved in making a hand-made flat cart to peddle our fish. It took us a couple of hours to get it lined up. Eating a hearty dinner of fresh fish, we set out on our new money-making scheme. Not being able to run the cart on the shore, we had to carry the fish from the oil drum, in potato sacks, over to the large wash tub we had nailed on the cart. After seizing about seventy-five pounds, we made for the road. It wasn't hard to find us, as every blue-assed fly in the universe was following us.

We found out the only time people would buy our fish was if they got us in the shade. The flies seemed not too lively there, but in the sun they formed a canopy overhead.

The fish were starting to smell and so we had to work fast. It wasn't long before we met some competitors. Although they had a nicer cart with a large wooden box in which the fish had been packed in ice, they weren't as fortunate as us. Our only trouble was with flies – theirs was with cats. Their refrigeration had broken down, and the ice had lasted no time in the heat. And they were having a lot of trouble with a wheel on their cart. The fish were nearly cooked, and the smell was unbearable.

Neighbours phoned the police about the fish set-up. They were alarmed about losing their cats. The wind being in the direction of the project, every cat and her kittens would smell that wonderful aroma and run in the direction of the scent. You wouldn't believe your eyes. Cats took over with their mournful cries. Bill and I continued on with our nearly-baked fish and our display of all-sized blue-assed flies haloed around the cart. We got rid of the remaining fish by throwing them in the river, went home, dressed a little, and saw the Western with change to spare.

Rinso Sausage

Brother Bill was the luckiest one in the bunch of us brothers for getting employment. I guess it was his good looks, and he was never as shy as the rest of us. When a brother got a job, we'd work where he did, whether wanted or not. We'd hang around with him until they hired one of us.

A small butcher shop was Bill's place of employment. The owner Dave was a humourous man and he liked Bill, and so as far as I was concerned, he had to like me too.

Groceries and meats were his main fare, and he had worked up a nice little business. The orders called in were delivered by me on a bicycle: Bill's bike. (Don't ask me where he got it; he had a habit of getting anything he wanted, even your prettiest girlfriend.) In the back of the store was a hall about ten feet long and four feet wide. Mounted on a bench was a sausage machine. It wasn't long before I learned to run it myself without Bill's help.

Bill, out front with Dave, had enough to do, and so I was left to make the sausages. Orders would come in giving us only three or four hours' notice to supply the hospital in town with fifty or sometimes a hundred pounds. Three times a week those orders would come in. Besides the hospital, the people in the town were crazy about Dave's sausages.

Wages for my work were paid by Bill, who received a six-day-work-week pay of four dollars, out of which my wage was one dollar. It was given with good intent, but if I didn't spend it right away, Bill would borrow it with little intention of paying it back. I'd never make a fuss, because it was such a pleasure just working at the store, with everything you wished for in life on the shelf. When Dave would go to dinner, I'd sample nearly everything in less than an hour. Dates, figs, prunes, boiled ham, bologna, chocolates, tomatoes, even a box of Exlax because of its candy look. Fruit and meat didn't hurt me much, but when it came to the Exlax, I had to cancel the bicycle deliveries. That was too much exercise for my already touchy large intestine.

One day, after a phone call from the hospital, Dave told me that they needed one hundred pounds of sausage. I began my duties. The first thing to do when an order came in was to start cutting. Bones were stripped. Meat that wasn't too red was cut into small pieces.

The unground meat –pieces of suet, heels of bologna – was placed in a large galvanized wash tub. From there I put it in the coarse grinder. After going through the grinder, it would find its way to another wash tub on the floor directly below the machine spout. Changing the machine grinding system to a finer grind, the coarse grind was brought to a very fine texture in no time. Sausage flour was then added to the second process, and water was poured in. Then began my muscle building. With sleeves rolled up I proceeded to mix. Every quarter of an hour Bill or Dave would come in to see how I was progressing as the hospital had given us a time limit. Everything was running smoothly. The new fine sawdust on the floors, back and front, gave my spirits a lift. After all this kneading of the meat, it was getting rather stuffy in the back store, and so I decided to give myself some fresh air. Hoisting the window under great strain, I upset the large Rinso box that we used to wash the utensils. Every chip from the box went into the mushy sausage mixture. (I think that's why they have remodelled the soap packages today, putting a perforated mouth on them instead of the old-fashioned type where you had to tear the whole top off.)

On my way down from the window and straddling the machine, my two rubber-booted feet went directly into the meat and drove the Rinso almost out of sight. Getting out of this predicament faster than I got in it, I could do nothing but put the empty box out of the way and cover up the Rinso with the mushy meat. I cleaned off my rubber boots as the phone in the front was ringing, praying Dave would answer it. He did, and so I beckoned to my brother fast.

I was having trouble trying to get Billy to understand about the Rinso. He was in a state of uproarious laughter, thinking I had just slipped into the mix; but when I dug into the centre and came up with pounds of soap chips, his face sobered. Most of the Rinso was dissolving and it was a frothy mess. We grabbed as much of it as we could and packed it in a rat hole in the back. After getting rid of the golden flakes, Bill and I hurled the meat into the machine, placed the sausage casings on the spout, grabbed the long links and began tying them in lots.

Laughing hysterically, we continued as a two-man team. Dave joined in the laughter, not knowing what had gone before.

It wasn't long before we had the hospital supper ready and bleached. The phone call said they would take half the order and the other half could be delivered tomorrow. The remainder was sold to customers in the town. It was the hospital's habit of telling you how they liked the sausage. Surprisingly, this time, they pronounced it "very tasty indeed".

A lady customer with a family of six came for her regular three pounds for a quarter. She lived over a mile away, and before closing time at 6 p.m., she arrived back again, saying they were different and she had enjoyed them so much. She bought another three pounds. So I guess the moral of the story is that the proof of the eating is in the mixing.

Nothing was said by Bill or me to Dave. But we kept a constant vigil on the obituaries and checked everyone who had died in the hospital that night, wishing we could have known what they had had for their last meal. It was a night of worry for me, but as time goes on you have a tendency to forget. The next morning, my first job was to cut up the bulk meat and process it through from pig's head to shiny, pretty clean sausages to finish up the hospital order. This batch didn't receive the complimentary remarks the first batch did. Now I'm not suggesting putting Rinso in your sausage, but what was it that drew the woman back? Why did the hospital remind us how good they were?

One night a few days later Bill and I went to clean up the store. I never knew what to eat; I guess I had tried everything before. But this night I felt like eating strawberry jam. I reached up and got a two-and-a-half pound bottle and spooned it all down.

That night I threw up strawberry jam, and Pa had the biggest scare of his life. He thought I was hemorrhaging and suggested we call the doctor immediately. Pa was quick to suggest the hospital. He was paying for it weekly through a check-off system they had in the mines. So I guess he was like the rest of the Scots, thinking not so much of me, but of the food to be saved with one out of the fold. Bill was trying desperately to discourage Pa from sending me there. The only transportation was Bill's bike or the neighbour's wheelbarrow, and so Bill managed to talk Pa out of sending me off that night. If Pa had had a car, or anyone else close by, I would have been rushed there, pumped out, and stuffed with my own Rinso sausage for breakfast.

There was another time when Pa would have liked to have put the four of us in hospital. It was a gloomy, blustery day in February, and Teedy, Murray, Bill, and I were studying our lessons in the "ghost-room" when all of a sudden—

But that's another tale and it seems I could go on forever telling stories about my boyhood, because as the auctioneer says when advertising a sale, "There are many items, just too numerous to mention."